Progressive Studio Pedagogy

Progressive Studio Pedagogy provides guidance to educators in all design fields by questioning processes and assumptions about teaching and learning, utilising examples from architecture, landscape architecture, and interior design.

Through a series of case studies, this book presents innovative approaches to learning and teaching in design studio. Traditionally, design education is perceived to be a process for acquiring skills and a site for developing creative potential. However, contemporary higher education is embracing issues that include widening participation, managing transition, and fostering independent learning and graduate employability. This book situates design learning within this varied context and offers insights into how to confront the challenge of facilitating learning through divergent contexts by presenting projects and courses that use a range of approaches that require students to think and act critically and evaluatively.

Progressive Studio Pedagogy presents new practices that readers can adapt into their own creative education, making it an ideal read for those interested in teaching design.

Charlie Smith is Reader in Creative Pedagogies at Liverpool John Moores University. His research focuses on learning and teaching in creative disciplines – and on assessment and feedback in particular – to enhance and enrich the student learning experience. Research projects he has led include studying students' perceptions of the design review, students' understanding and uptake of feedback, and students' expectations and experience of higher education. He has also innovated ways in which students' studio project work can inform research projects, creating collaborative partnerships with them.

Routledge Focus on Design Pedagogy
Series Editor: Graham Cairns

The Routledge Focus on Design Pedagogy series provides the reader with the latest scholarship for instructors who educate designers. The series publishes research from across the globe and covers areas as diverse as beginning design and foundational design, architecture, product design, interior design, fashion design, landscape architecture, urban design, and architectural conservation and historic preservation. By making these studies available to the worldwide academic community, the series aims to promote quality design education.

Fluid Space and Transformational Learning
Kyriaki Tsoukala

Progressive Studio Pedagogy
Examples from Architecture and Allied Design Fields
Edited by Charlie Smith

For more information about this series, please visit: www.routledge.com/architecture/series/RFDP

Progressive Studio Pedagogy

Examples from Architecture
and Allied Design Fields

Edited by Charlie Smith

Routledge
Taylor & Francis Group

LONDON AND NEW YORK

First published 2021
by Routledge
2 Park Square, Milton Park, Abingdon, Oxon OX14 4RN

and by Routledge
52 Vanderbilt Avenue, New York, NY 10017

Routledge is an imprint of the Taylor & Francis Group, an informa business

British Library Cataloguing-in-Publication Data
A catalogue record for this book is available from the British Library

Library of Congress Cataloging-in-Publication Data
A catalog record for this book has been requested

ISBN: 978-0-36764-9-135 (hbk)
ISBN: 978-1-00312-6-911 (ebk)

Typeset in Times New Roman
by Apex CoVantage, LLC

Contents

Illustrations

Figures

Tables

Boxes

Acknowledgements

On behalf of the chapter authors and myself, I would like to offer deepest thanks to Grace Harrison and Julia Pollacco at Routledge/Taylor and Francis and to Graham Cairns at Architecture, Media, Politics, Society (AMPS) for their support and guidance during the development of this book. I would also like to thank the external reviewers of the proposal for their insightful feedback and suggestions. Kindest thanks are also offered to the Art Gallery of South Australia for permission to reproduce the image in Chapter 2 from their collection and to the students whose work and commentary is reproduced throughout this book.

Contributors

Sean Burns
Ball State University, USA
Sean Burns is an assistant professor of architecture at Ball State University specialising in architectural design, with an emphasis on foundations of design and beginner architectural education, as well as structural principles and behavioural analysis. He holds a bachelor of architecture degree from Kent State University and a post-professional master of architecture degree from the University of Pennsylvania. His current research concentrates on how the conditions of a site, both above and beyond the demarcation of the earth's surface, and qualitative substance composition might be influential agents throughout the architectural design process.

Magda Fourie-Malherbe
University of Stellenbosch, South Africa
Magda Fourie-Malherbe is a professor emerita of curriculum studies in the Faculty of Education, Stellenbosch University. She holds qualifications from the University of the Free State and Stellenbosch University and has worked for more than thirty years at public higher education institutions in South Africa as a lecturer, academic developer, researcher, supervisor and administrator. Her research includes higher education governance, leadership and management, teaching and learning, and transformation. She has authored and co-authored more than forty contributions to scholarly journals, books and research reports and been a guest lecturer at universities in Botswana, Uganda and China.

Gerhard Griesel
Cape Peninsula University of Technology, South Africa
Gerhard Griesel has over seventeen years of experience in landscape architecture and is currently a lecturer in the Diploma in Landscape Architecture programme at the Cape Peninsula University of Technology (CPUT). Graduating with a master's degree in landscape architecture from the University of Pretoria, he started in private practice immediately after graduation

and started his own landscape architecture firm in 2006. He expanded his career into academia, joining the lecturing team of CPUT to further the landscape design profession. He completed his PhD in curriculum studies in the Department of Education at the University of Stellenbosch and created a design skill set framework for landscape architecture students.

Charlie Smith
Liverpool John Moores University, UK
Charlie Smith is a reader in creative pedagogies at Liverpool John Moores University. His research focuses on learning and teaching in creative disciplines – and on assessment and feedback in particular – to enhance and enrich the student learning experience. Research projects he has led include studying students' perceptions of the design review, students' understanding and uptake of feedback, and students' expectations and experience of higher education. He has also innovated ways in which students' studio project work can inform research projects, creating collaborative partnerships with them.

Andrew R. Tripp
Texas A&M University, USA
Andrew R. Tripp is an assistant professor in architecture at Texas A&M University and has degrees in architecture from the University of Pennsylvania (PhD) and the Cooper Union (BArch). Before joining the Department of Architecture at Texas A&M, he taught at the Cooper Union, University of Pennsylvania, University of the Arts in Philadelphia and Mississippi State University. His research focuses on the intersection of architecture, education and globalisation, with an emphasis on twentieth-century architectural history and theory. His current research records, reveals and reinterprets the impact of globalisation on the architecture of educational facilities since the Second World War.

Anika van Aswegen
University of Pretoria, South Africa
Anika van Aswegen is a lecturer in the department of architecture, University of Pretoria, specialising in interior. She has a master's by research degree in interior architecture from the same institution and is currently engaged with her PhD. Her research interest combines design pedagogy with dynamic conditions of inhabitation related to urban interiors, with emphasis on human-centred design and 'interiority'. Other ways of creative inquiry inform her teaching methodology, especially approaches from the creative arts and social sciences. She coordinates and facilitates an interdisciplinary interface design studio, teaches design theory and is a reviewer for an international journal.

Introduction

Charlie Smith, Editor

Design studio pedagogy is an area of study that is diverse and growing. Interest in this field has intensified over the past decade and is expected to continue to flourish as creative professions evolve with increasing pace and higher education continually transforms. This book is premised on the argument that challenging orthodoxy should be an intrinsic dimension of creative pedagogy. It offers insights to educators in all design fields whilst questioning traditional processes and assumptions about both teaching and learning. Progressive, in the context of this book, means that studio pedagogy should continually question its methods, embrace avant-garde practices and align itself with the often challenging and constantly evolving context that higher education lies within. The central narrative is that teaching in creative disciplines should itself be characterised by original and imaginative methods, ones which support students' transition into higher education, nurture their creative skills and critical thinking, and enrich their learning experience.

Using case studies from the fields of architecture, landscape architecture and interior architecture, this book reflects on teaching strategies that readers can adapt into their own teaching practices and inspire them to similarly reimagine elements of their curriculum. Drawing from related fields in spatial design means there is significant crossover in the strategies described and they are all transferable. There is focus on important issues in contemporary design pedagogy, including enhancing design skill sets, critical thinking, human-centred and research-based design processes, and nurturing evaluative judgment. These are captured and discussed through new perspectives in different contexts. Collectively, the case studies include examples of studio practice from across all three years of undergraduate education. This book will be of interest to anyone involved in teaching design, especially within spatial design disciplines. It will also be of interest to academics and researchers in higher education pedagogy – particularly in creative disciplines and including graduate research students in the field of design pedagogy – as well as curricular designers, programme administrators, and professional bodies overseeing education and professions in the creative industries.

Contemporary higher education faces a complex web of issues. For example, massification and widening participation rightly demand increasing recognition that students arrive at university from remarkably diverse backgrounds and with widely ranging skill sets and abilities, placing the facilitation and support of students' transition into tertiary education in the fore. Smit argues that massification has brought the university to a place where it is not ready to deal with the diversity it faces and that the dominant deficit model of thinking needs to be replaced with more suitable responses to diversity in the student body.[1] This book presents different ways to nurture the enculturation of students into a community of practice within the field of design learning. Fostering students' capability to learn autonomously has long been a key objective in preparing them for their life after graduation.[2] However, with the continuing commodification of higher education, not least due to increasing fee regimes, educational value is also being placed under the spotlight,[3] factors influencing which include teaching quality, course content and graduate employability.[4] This book situates design learning within this milieu and offers examples of how design curricula can nurture students' transition, enrich their creative learning experience, and enhance their critical judgement skills.

Reflecting on their own studio practices, in each chapter the authors present an innovative approach they have taken in relation to a fundamental theme in design learning. The chapters follow the sequence of the creative teaching and learning process itself. Starting from enculturating students into a creative community of practice via their existing skill sets, the book moves through supporting the development of students' critical thinking skills at the beginning of their design education, to alternative approaches to learning and teaching within the design studio, finishing with nurturing students' capability to make evaluative judgements over the quality of the work they have produced. However, these are also stand-alone case studies, meaning that the chapters can be read in any sequence.

Recognising that students arrive in higher education from diverse backgrounds and the importance of supporting transition, in Chapter 1, Gerhard Griesel, Programme Coordinator in Landscape Architecture at Cape Peninsula University of Technology, and Magda Fourie-Malherbe, Professor Emerita of Curriculum Studies in the Faculty of Education at Stellenbosch University, discuss a framework for enhancing design skill sets which was applied in a landscape architecture studio. Teaching students through their preferred skill sets supported them to experience learning in ways they are most comfortable with, but it also challenged them to learn in other ways.

The argument is made that multiple modal entry points to design shift attention away from underdeveloped skills as barriers to learning, proactively engage the interest of students, and facilitate the development of design skills and cognition of domain specific knowledge.

The second chapter also addresses skills at the outset of design education and confronts the challenge of facilitating the transfer of learning between divergent contexts. Andrew R. Tripp, Assistant Professor in Architecture at Texas A&M University, presents a course design in which writing in studio becomes a means for students to think and act critically. He posits that students entering a design studio are willing and capable learners, but often are unable to transfer learning from one context to another and proposes that a most robust mechanism for developing the skills to transfer knowledge between learning contexts already exists in a student's natural language. Prompting them to improve their ability to manipulate language through writing provides a concrete opportunity to abstract and transfer learning between contexts. Exploring this through the example of an architectural design studio, this chapter rebuffs commonplace arguments against writing in the design studio and describes an approach for integrating it into curriculum development.

Chapters 3 and 4 similarly rethink traditional approaches within the design studio. This is done first by exploring other forms of critical inquiry through activities in which the user becomes a spatial participant and, second, by challenging the engrained notion that site is invariable and describing projects that provoke collaborative exploration between architecture and its environment. In Chapter 3, Anika van Aswegen, a lecturer specialising in interior in the Department of Architecture at the University of Pretoria, explores other ways of creative and critical inquiry to diversify conventional design methods in studio. She explores the use of a speculative workshop as an empirical case study that is inserted 'as disruption' in an undergraduate design project. This methodology aimed to raise awareness of a human-centred approach by uncovering deeper design responses that prioritised users and real-life scenarios. In this case, it was done through the example of an interior architecture project and emphasised 'spatial agency' over physical architectural solutions. Analysis revealed the significance of human-centred values within the design process, with 'empathy' the most challenging of those to sustain beyond the workshop. She describes the approach as probing transformative development of students towards a new praxis, as citizen designers.

Chapter 4 explores how students can approach design as a flexible process of mediation between variables. Sean Burns, Assistant Professor of Architecture at Ball State University, observes that students are often taught to operate sequentially within the design process by observing, recording and then responding to its existing conditions. He argues that this procedure, while beneficial in teaching students to acknowledge and appreciate the contextual environment for design, can be misguided as it emphasises certain parameters as given, invariable constraints. Examining a methodological approach to design that departs from the traditional sequence of observe, record and respond, he encourages students to enter a responsive dialogue between designed object and context throughout the design process. Using the example of architectural design, this chapter argues for a reconsideration of architecture and the conditions of project sites as malleable, accommodating bodies.

The final chapter discusses nurturing students' capability in making evaluative judgments, thereby transforming a hidden aspect of the design curriculum into an explicit one. Developing students' evaluative judgement – the capability to make decisions about quality in their own work and that of others – is a key skill: one required both during their time at university and for lifelong learning in an increasingly uncertain employment landscape. This chapter critically appraises two strategies for nourishing such judgement that have been trailed in an undergraduate architecture programme at a post ninety-two UK university and which are particularly suited to design-related disciplines: student peer review and using exemplars as a medium through which to discuss standards and dimensions of quality. It is argued that nurturing evaluative judgement should be an explicit learning objective in higher education and not a tacit process where it is assumed that students will develop this capability through osmosis.

Interest in learning to think creatively is spreading beyond design disciplines, not least given the increasingly rapid evolution and uncertain context of graduate employment. In his book *Out of Our Minds: The Power of Being Creative*, Ken Robinson proposes that the skills and qualities that are essential to meet the challenges of an increasingly complex world are creativity, cultural understanding, communication, collaboration and problem solving.[5] He maintains that not only can all disciplines be creative and include dimensions of aesthetics, elegance and beauty, but creativity often comes about through interaction between multidisciplinary ways of seeing things.[6] He notes, however, that due to massification, increasing student numbers and resource limitations, the demand for these skills comes at a time when higher education institutions are least able to develop and provide them.[7] This highlights the significance of developing progressive creative thinking and learning processes across all disciplines, and not limited to those within the art and design school, but also the challenges that might be faced in doing so.

The landscapes of higher education and graduate employment are changing rapidly and the forms they will take, even within the near future, are at best uncertain and impossible to foresee. Few would argue that the key objective of design education is to spark students' curiosity and nourish their creative imagination, skills and thinking. Similarly, there is an onus on these disciplines to embrace creativity and innovation in their own learning, teaching and evaluation methods. Students within all disciplines must learn the skills to be adaptive, resilient, independent and imaginative. Robinson argues that education needs transforming in ways that address the challenges of contemporary living and working, with a systematic approach cultivating imagination, creativity and innovation, and nurturing relationships between disciplines.[8] Learning and teaching in creative fields have much to offer the evolution of tertiary education across the sector to embrace and meet these new challenges.

Notes

1 Reneé Smit, "Towards a Clearer Understanding of Student Disadvantage in Higher Education: Problematising Deficit Thinking," *Higher Education Research and Development* 31, no. 3 (2012): 374 and 378, accessed April 30, 2020, doi:10. 1080/07294360.2011.634383.
2 Liz Thomas, Robert Jones and James Ottaway, *Effective Practice in the Design of Directed Independent Learning Opportunities: Summary of the Main Research Report* (York: Higher Education Academy, March 12, 2015), 8, accessed May 1, 2020, www.advance-he.ac.uk/knowledge-hub/effective-practice-design-directed-independent-learning-opportunities.
3 Department for Education, *Independent Panel Report to the Review of Post-18 Education and Funding* (London: Her Majesty's Stationary Office, May 30, 2019), 81–91, accessed March 31, 2020, www.gov.uk/government/publications/post-18-review-of-education-and-funding-independent-panel-report.
4 Jonathan Neves and Nick Hillman, *Student Academic Experience Survey 2019* (York and Oxford: Advance HE and Higher Education Policy Institute, June 2019), 13, accessed April 30, 2020, www.hepi.ac.uk/wp-content/uploads/2019/06/Student-Academic-Experience-Survey-2019.pdf.
5 Ken Robinson, *Out of Our Minds: The Power of Being Creative*, Third Edition (Chichester, UK: Wiley, 2017), 9.
6 Ibid., 3, 159 and 183.
7 Ibid., 55.
8 Ibid., 209–10 and 237.

Bibliography

Department for Education. *Independent Panel Report to the Review of Post-18 Education and Funding*. London: Her Majesty's Stationary Office, May 30, 2019. Accessed March 31, 2020. www.gov.uk/government/publications/post-18-review-of-education-and-funding-independent-panel-report.
Neves, Jonathan, and Nick Hillman. *Student Academic Experience Survey 2019*. York and Oxford: Advance HE and Higher Education Policy Institute, June, 2019.

Accessed April 30, 2020. www.hepi.ac.uk/wp-content/uploads/2019/06/Student-Academic-Experience-Survey-2019.pdf.

Robinson, Ken. *Out of Our Minds: The Power of Being Creative.* Third Edition. Chichester, UK: Wiley, 2017.

Smit, Reneé. "Towards a Clearer Understanding of Student Disadvantage in Higher Education: Problematising Deficit Thinking." *Higher Education Research and Development* 31, no. 3 (2012): 369–80. Accessed April 30, 2020. doi:10.1080/07 294360.2011.634383.

Thomas, Liz, Robert Jones, and James Ottaway. *Effective Practice in the Design of Directed Independent Learning Opportunities: Summary of the Main Research Report.* York: Higher Education Academy, March 12, 2015. Accessed May 1, 2020. www.advance-he.ac.uk/knowledge-hub/effective-practice-design-directed-independent-learning-opportunities.

1 A framework for enhancing the design skill sets of landscape architecture students

Gerhard Griesel and Magda Fourie-Malherbe

Introduction

Internationally the imperatives for access and fair chances of success have given rise to criticism of undergraduate design programmes for being inaccessible and for catering only to a narrow group of students with specific skill sets and design aptitudes.[1] The mismatch or gap in design skill sets that the majority of students in undergraduate design programmes experience is widened by low design exposure and underpreparedness to study this specialist discipline. This is a universal trait of students registered for design-based qualifications at higher education institutions internationally.[2] Current design teaching also contributes to this gap, because of the inappropriate assumptions about students' prior knowledge that do not take sufficient account of the wide range of educational preparedness of students and what they require to bridge the transitions from school to university and between various phases of undergraduate study.

The primary focus of landscape architecture design programmes is on developing skill sets through disciplinary content. 'Skill sets' is an umbrella term that includes various commonly used terms such as ability (skill to do something), aptitude (natural ability), competency (the ability to do something well), intelligence (ability to learn and understand) and creativity (the ability to make new things).[3] Although novice design students may initially be unable to understand the design process or to communicate these ideas, Cidre,[4] Moore[5] and Cubukcu and Cetintahra[6] argue that design skills are not inherent and can be developed. Subscribing to the view that creative potential is a combination of various skills that can be learned and taught, this chapter introduces a framework to enhance the design skill sets of landscape architecture students.

Design as a set of skills

Cross posits that design knowledge is a "designerly way of knowing."[7] From this broad definition of design knowledge, different studies in design elaborate on a 'designerly way of knowing.' Authors like Goldschmidt and

Sebba[8] and Casakin and Goldschmidt[9] explored design aptitude, Cross[10] examined the personality traits of designers, others looked at design process and methods,[11] and some at the nature of design.[12] Lawson hypothesises that design is a highly complex and sophisticated skill.[13] D'souza and Chandrasekhara elaborate on this hypothesis by arguing that design cannot be restricted to a unique skill, but that it should rather be interpreted as a flexible framework that consists of multiple abilities that designers intentionally use to achieve desired goals in specific design scenarios.[14] Thus, the designer must become an 'integrator' of various skills and knowledge.[15] This demands a wide array of skill sets, for example, spatial visualisation, logical thinking, emotional reflection, linguistic ability and interpersonal skills.[16]

D'souza and Chandrasekhara further argue that identifying the composite of skill sets for designers could firstly contribute to making design learning more inclusive, as differences in skills levels, weaknesses and strengths of students could be clearly identified, and secondly, such an approach could support the recognition and appreciation of individual differences and approaches in design.[17] D'souza suggests organising design skills into four thematic sets, referred to as design skills sets.[18] The themes include:

- Emotional design skill set:

  How a student feels can profoundly shape how they think. For example, emotions can promote learning by capturing and holding attention.[19] D'souza suggests that, when there is insufficient information to make logical judgments, a designer will rely on emotions and instinct.[20] Goldschmidt and Sebba confirm this by stating that designers use new and unexpected combinations of existing knowledge, items in memory and new information superimposed on them.[21] Skills that involve emotions are intrapersonal intelligence (personal emotions) and interpersonal intelligence (another's emotions).

- Sensory design skill set:

  Designers interact constantly with the environment surrounding them.[22] Furthermore, designers' creative self-confidence is influenced by how they perceive their environment to be either restrictive or encouraging. This will influence the individual's potential for creative behaviours and creativity displayed.[23] Skills that are associated with such external senses include kinesthetic intelligence (visualising or experiencing the movement of the body in relation with the external environment) and naturalistic intelligence (visualising and experiencing nature and natural phenomena).[24]

- Logical design skill set:

  These skills refer to how designers understand and apply abstract symbols/formulae, formal logical thinking, deciphering codes, numerical calculations and problem solving.[25] Nazidizaji et al. argue that design is an open-ended problem-solving process and the functions of design skills support designers' cognitive abilities.[26] Skills that involve logic are logical-mathematical intelligence (working with numbers and geometry as well as solving problems) and spatial intelligence (understanding symbols and identifying and designing formal strategies).

- Ideational design skill set:

  Ideational/depictive skills allow for the visualisation and representation of concepts, ideas and spaces. This skill set has the strongest connections to design, because these skills involve both the medium and product of designing.[27] Lawson observes that there are many types of thinking and concludes that reasoning and imagining are probably the most important to designers.[28] Spatial intelligence includes the ability to perceive the visual world accurately and to transform and modify initial perceptions via mental imagery.

This appreciation of a composite of skill sets for designers reduces the overt emphasis on graphical skills and form making by recognising the importance of skills such as problem-solving, spatial sensitivity, interpersonal and linguistic skills that are critical in dealing with real-world design situations.

The challenge

The peculiar character of the landscape architectural profession requires landscape architects to be familiar with a wide range of knowledge fields, extending from the field of natural sciences to that of artistic creativity.[29] The complexity of design tasks requires individuals to have a wide array of skills, including spatial visualisation, problem-solving, verbal, communication, and interpersonal skills. Yet design education today seems to be limiting skills to form manipulation and graphical skills. These latter skills, although essential to design, predict only a part of a designer's application in real-world contexts.

The transition process into higher education, referred to by, amongst others, Botes and Khan,[30] places the first-year student in a vulnerable position. The relocation of a student from their home into an unfamiliar environment and lifestyle is a huge challenge in the absence of social support previously provided by the family and/or familiar social context. This requires adjustment through establishing new friendships and a redefinition of individual identity construction.[31]

Students of diverse and poor socioeconomic backgrounds are even more vulnerable in the higher education context.[32] Design students from a poor socioeconomic background are particularly prone to incompletion of studies due to the unlikelihood of them having been exposed to design disciplines, as a result of subject offering limitations in state-resourced schools.[33] Briggs, Clark and Hall warn that these difficulties in transition could lead to students deregistering, which is particularly problematic in the case of those students who aspire to transform their socioeconomic status through higher education.[34] The role of the educator in addressing the threats of incomplete studies is therefore crucial.[35] The design skill set framework explicated here is an attempt to assist design students, particularly those from disadvantaged backgrounds, to cope more effectively with the transition from school to higher education by enhancing their design skill sets in innovative ways.

Design skill set enhancement framework

The design skill set enhancement framework was developed through the exploration of existing principles of teaching and learning in design education as well as the creation of the design skill set modal agencies and the design knowledge semiotic process, as illustrated in Figure 1.1. The three components of the framework are explicated here.

Existing design education principles

Design education should encourage individuality of interpretation and expression by creating environments that allow for different perspectives and multiple solutions. These environments must cater for how students perceive themselves, how they construct and share knowledge, and how they understand and apply the design process to resolve problems and develop creative outcomes. Gajda, Beghetto and Karwowski remark that creative learning requires opportunities for students to engage with new and different perspectives and to have opportunities to share and receive feedback on their own perspectives.[36] Herrington and Herrington observe that traditional approaches in higher education have not resulted in appropriate learning outcomes.[37] The challenge lies in how effectively and substantively an alignment between higher education teaching and learning and the way learning in real-life settings occurs can be achieved.[38]

The following principles highlight some of the influences that may affect a student-centred, realistic and effective learning environment in design education: self-efficacy and environmental influences, authentic contextual

Design Skill Set Enhancement Framework

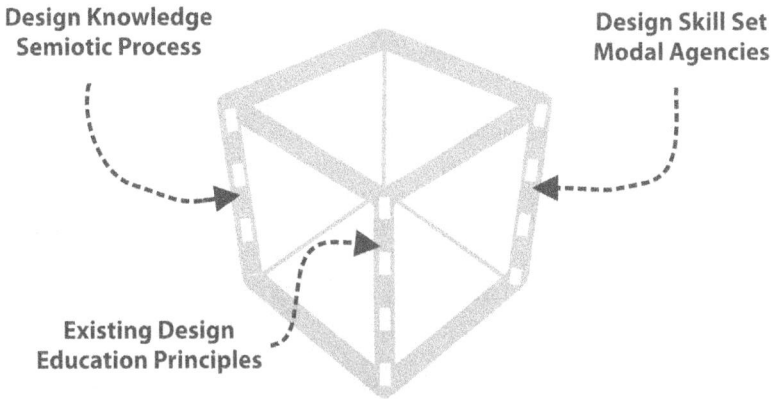

**Design Knowledge
Semiotic Process**

**Design Skill Set
Modal Agencies**

**Existing Design
Education Principles**

Figure 1.1 Design skill set enhancement framework

environments, collaborative learning environments, analogical reasoning and process of interpretation.

Self-efficacy and environmental influences

Looking beyond the basic definitions of creativity, some creativity theorists have recently highlighted the importance of individuals' perceptions of their own creative competency. Diliello, Houghton and Dawley posit that an individual will experience creative expression when that person perceives that their work environment supports creativity.[39] Research by Gajda, Beghetto and Karwowski indicates the importance of affective support when it comes to behaviours associated with creative learning, that is, a type of 'emotional scaffolding.'[40] This is also applicable to the learning environment. Plucker recommends that the learning environment should address misconceptions of creativity and how students see themselves, other people and creativity as a construct.[41] Thus, establishing an emotionally supportive and caring environment could provide the psychological safety net necessary for students to take the risks required for creative learning and expression.

By enhancing the individual's self-efficacy,[42] a creative self-confidence can be developed that would encourage the individual's willingness to take the necessary risks to be innovative. It is, however, also important to note that when individuals perceive themselves as having creative potential, but do not acknowledge the ability to use this potential, they will be less likely to engage in creative behaviour.[43] Developing creative self-efficacy hence becomes an important principle in design education.

Authentic contextual environments

Reeve et al. theorise that to establish a contextual and complex learning environment that is purposeful and motivational, the context must be all-embracing.[44] The context needs to incorporate not only a physical environment that will reflect the manner in which knowledge will be used but also a large variety of resources to facilitate the evaluation of different perspectives.[45]

Puckett and Reese observe that many courses miss this opportunity by removing ordinary, real-life experiences from course materials.[46] In many cases, generalised theoretical principles and skills are taught rather than situation-specific capabilities. When learning and context are separated, knowledge itself is seen by students as the final product of education rather than the tool to be used to solve problems.[47] Bereiter notes that declarative knowledge should be seen as a first step in gaining cognitive skills, which needs to be followed by a procedural stage in which knowledge is demonstrated in the actual behaviour of students.[48] In the process of gaining cognitive skills and moving to the procedural stage, context plays an important role in determining how a problem will be perceived, as well as providing support and strategies a student will use to solve it.[49] As a possible model of instruction to address this process of knowledge development, Resnick proposes 'bridging apprenticeships' that were designed to bridge the gap between theoretical learning in the classroom and the real-life application of knowledge in the working environment.[50] This model was further developed into a theory of situated cognition or situated learning by Brown, Collins, Duguid and Seely,[51] incorporating the notion of acquiring knowledge and skills in contexts that reflect the way knowledge will be applied in real-life situations. Authentic contextual teaching and learning environments facilitate the process of knowledge development by bridging the gap between theoretical knowledge concepts and the understanding and real-life application of that theoretical knowledge.

Collaborative learning environments

Collaboration is an ongoing effort and mutual engagement of all participants to cooperatively understand and maintain a shared conception of a problem through simultaneous and coordinated activities.[52] Collaboration and the opportunity to collaboratively construct knowledge are important elements in the construction of authentic creative learning environments,[53] as the interaction between individual divergent practices and shared knowledge development learning activities is enhanced.[54] Creative learning environments should be extended beyond the concepts of physical learning spaces[55] and include psychosocial and pedagogical elements,[56] as well as the influences of external environments and social interactions. Additionally, Addison et al. advocate for the extension of learning environments into the outdoor setting as this will foster creative development.[57] There is a positive correlation between these authentic creative environments and students' construction of knowledge, especially for lower-achieving students.[58] Wiles et al. suggest that outdoor time and space are seen as more 'owned' by students.[59] The 'indoor' classroom is perceived to be individually focused, whereas outdoor activities encourage more collaborative learning. Collaborative learning environments support the co-construction of knowledge and mediate the creative learning process towards a shared understanding and development of domain-specific knowledge and skills.

Analogical reasoning

Analogical reasoning is an effective cognitive mechanism that assists with the understanding of new knowledge by linking the 'unfamiliar' with the 'familiar.'[60] Analogies transfer relational knowledge from a known situation (usually referred to as the source or base) to a situation that needs explanation (referred to as the target), where at least one of the elements is not known.[61] Through the process of analogical mapping, a system of relations concerning the central properties of that knowledge is created and transferred from the base to the target situation. Identifying the similarity between possible relations in the target situation and known relations in the source situation leads to the creation of an analogy.[62] According to Goldschmidt and Smolkov,[63] the process of ideation, that is, idea or concept generation, is possible due to the identification of visual clues, which is supported by the interactive dialogue that designers establish between available external sources and internal representations. These external sources can be visual and/or verbal stimuli.

Visual stimuli or visual analogies assist with the definition of the problem and the clarification of ideas,[64] enhance the quality of design solutions,[65] improve design knowledge and skills,[66] and develop creativity.[67] On the other hand, verbal stimuli or verbal analogies enhance originality and creativity of designs and the generation of a large number of innovative ideas.[68] Both types of analogies contribute to the originality and aesthetic value of the final design outcome.[69] Analogical reasoning is important in the early stages of the design process, when the development of concepts and ideas affects the design decisions taken later.

Process of interpretation

The American philosopher C. S. Peirce developed a semiotic paradigm that describes how people construct an understanding of reality.[70] This paradigm helps us understand how signs (such as words) acquire their meanings (become concepts) and how those meanings are subsequently 'updated.'

The process of semiosis is based on three elements: a sign, an object and an interpretant. Through the process of semiosis, the sign acquires meaning for the interpretant by association with the object. The interpretant allocates meaning to the sign when it comes into physical contact (sees, hears, tastes or smells) with it. The interpretant, through the interpretation process, develops an understanding of what the sign stands for and connects it to the object.[71]

Objects can be classified into two categories, namely mediate and immediate objects. Mediate objects are the actual real objects to which the sign refers. For instance, the word 'rose' refers to a flowery shrub with, for example, green leaves and red flowers. However, to know there is a link between the two, you would picture or think about this real shrub, the rose. This mental representation of the object is the immediate object.[72]

There are three types of signs (representamen): the icon, the index and the symbol. An icon resembles or attempts to replicate the object by looking, sounding, tasting, smelling or feeling like it. A typical example of an icon is a photograph. A symbol has an arbitrary relationship with the object it represents. It does not look, sound, taste, smell or feel like the object. The link between the object and a symbol has to be learned. For example, the word 'rose' bears no resemblance to the real rose. Index or indexical sign has a causative link with the object, for example, smoke is an index of fire, and the indexical sign is caused directly by the object.[73]

According to Nadin, design principles are semiotic in nature.[74] To design means to structure systems of signs in such a way as to make the achievement of human goals possible: communication (as a form of social interaction), engineering (as a form of applied technical rationality) and business (as a form of shared efficiency).

The second component of the design skill set enhancement framework is the design knowledge semiotic process.

Design knowledge semiotic process

Knowledge, and specifically design knowledge, is differentiated by Lawson and Dorst as episodic (experimental) knowledge and semantic (theoretical) knowledge.[75] Design knowledge, in particular, is heavily dependent on episodic knowledge, especially episodic processes of meaning making.[76] Design educators are constantly challenged by how to transfer design knowledge to students and how to stimulate new insights within them.[77]

The design knowledge semiotic process (DKSP), influenced by both the analogical reasoning process of transferring relational knowledge from the 'familiar' to the 'unfamiliar' and Peirce's semiotic paradigm,[78] addresses this challenge by placing the focus on the semiotic meaning-making process. It includes the three elements of semiosis (sign, interpretant and object), but expands on the interpretation process amongst the mediate object, the sign and the immediate object. The mediate object represents a theoretical concept in design knowledge, the sign represents the interpretation process the interpretant must go through, and the immediate object represents the transferred mental representation of the theoretical concept. Although these processes of analogical reasoning and semiosis have been extensively implemented in various design education contexts,[79] what is original in this framework is the co-implementation of both processes in a domain-specific context and, more importantly, the methodical, step-by-step transference of a theoretical concept to a conceptual or mental representation. Stein refers to this sequential interpretation process as 'semiotic chains',[80] where teaching and learning occur through the ongoing creation and mediation of signs. Figure 1.2 provides a visual explanation of the elements and hierarchical levels of the DKSP, as well as the steps that indicate the procedural link between levels.

These steps are the practical activities that facilitate the creation of the cognitive links amongst the elements. They must be implemented in an authentic, context-specific environment to facilitate semiotic transference. The steps are facilitated by a set of four design skill set modal agencies, as discussed in the next session.

The interpretation process, that is, creating the sign, consists of the following elements:

* *Object*: a theoretical concept,

  for example, the basic design principle of symmetry.

* *Icon*: the direct presentation of the mediate object within a highly context-specific environment,

  for example, a plant leaf with a symmetrical vein structure.

* *Direct symbol*: the representation of the icon into a contextualised symbol within the same highly context-specific environment,

  for example, a sketch of the plant leaf.

* *Abstract symbol:* the representation of the contextualised symbol into a decontextualised abstract symbol,

  for example, the Mercedes Benz motor crest.

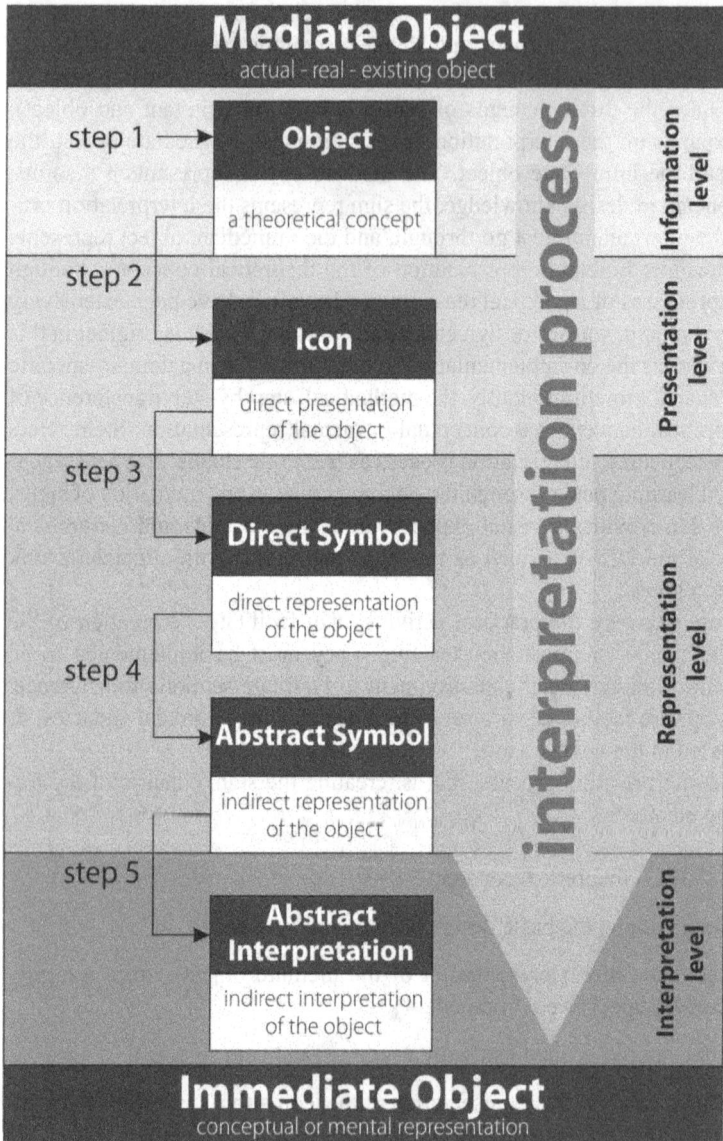

Figure 1.2 Design knowledge semiotic process

- *Abstract artefact*: the implementation of the abstract symbol into various contextual design requirements,

    for example, a landscape plan of a courtyard that is symmetrical.

The four hierarchical levels of the interpretation process are the following:

- *Information level*

    This is the least complex and occupies the lowest level of conceptual and methodological sophistication. The main function is holding the information until needed, that is, recording and storage of information.

- *Presentation level*

    This represents a denotative level of meaning, that is, not going beyond the direct meaning of the sign. The main function in this phase is presenting the information to others through showing and describing.

- *Representation level*

    This level embodies a construction of understanding of information that is re-presented through the presentation or representation of selected ideas, information and knowledge in a specific contextual environment.

- *Interpretation level*

    The process of creation and generation of design artefacts goes further than just drawing from informational, presentational and representational perspectives. The process culminates in an interpretation or translation that implicitly or explicitly explains the meaning of the information through various contextual environments.

Design skill set modal agencies

Gardner's multiple intelligence theory not only identifies eight relatively autonomous intelligences but also describes how individuals use these intelligences in the ways in which they take information in, retain and manipulate that information, and demonstrate their understanding of it to themselves and others.[81] Underwriting this theory, Newfield suggests a move away from previous 'monomodal approaches' to teaching and learning, with their focus on language as the primary mode of learning and assessment, towards the inclusion of more concrete, material, sensory and bodily practices.[82] According to Newfield, multimodality and multimodal pedagogies are founded upon the idea that meanings are made, disseminated and interpreted through many representational resources or modes such as image, sound, music, gesture, space, colour, facial expression, body posture and movement.[83] Kress and Selander emphasise that modal agency acts as a prompt for someone who engages with it to interpret (it or) part of it in the light of their interest and semiotic resources.[84] The four modal agencies, indicated in Table 1.1, act as facilitators for the enhancement of the four design skill sets in a multimodal teaching and learning environment. Each modal agency correlates to a specific design skill set, and each agency consists of specific meaning-making or semiotic tools that support the enhancement of that specific design skill set. In the process of defining the modal agency specific semiotic tools, design skill set attributes[85] were transcribed into modal entry points. Serematakis defines these entry points as senses or "meaning generating apparatuses" operating beyond consciousness and intention; they are inner states of feeling, relativised, contradicted or confirmed by embodied acts, gestures or sensory effects.[86] The modal entry points have the potential to hold in tension

Table 1.1 Design skill set developmental alignment

Required Design Skill Sets	Design Skill Set Modal Agencies and Semiotic Tools	Existing Design Education Principles
Ideational Skills	Ideational modal agencies: 1. Theoretical content course material 2. Verbal presentation 3. Direct presentation 4. Indirect representation	Ideational modal agencies: 1. Theoretical content course material 2. Verbal presentation 3. Direct presentation 4. Indirect representation
Sensory Skills	Sensory modal agencies: 1. Natural iconic presentation 2. Kinesthetic drawing 3. Kinesthetic expression	1. Self-efficacy and environmental influences 2. Authentic contextual environment 3. Collaborative learning environments 4. Analogical reasoning
Logical Skills	Logical modal agencies: 1. Logical iconic presentation 2. Logical symbolic representation 3. Logical interpretation	1. Authentic contextual environment 2. Collaborative learning environments
Emotional Skills	Emotional modal agencies: 1. Group work 2. Friends/peers 3. Individual 4. Self-study	1. Self-efficacy and environmental influences 2. Collaborative learning environments

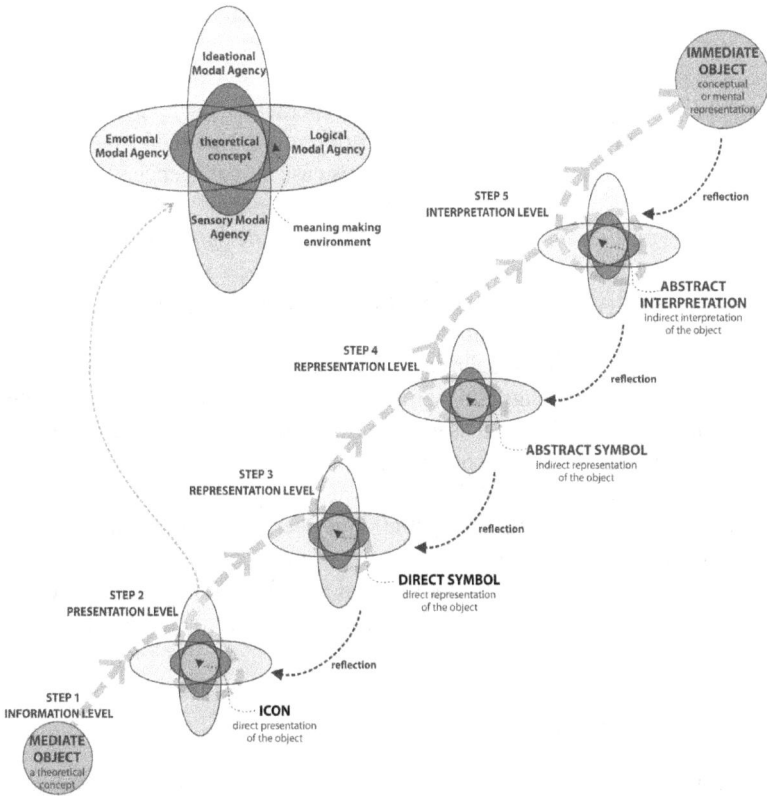

Figure 1.3 Framework for the modal agency meaning making

access to dominant pedagogies while incorporating the rich variety of representational resources.[87]

In the next section, we explain how the design skill set framework merges the two components, that is, the DKSP and the design skill set modal agencies, into the modal agency meaning-making process. Figure 1.3 illustrates not only the modal agency meaning-making process but also how each agency-specific intervention aligns to specific steps in the DKSP.

Modal agency meaning-making process

The affordance of a social semiotic and multimodal approach to learning is the recognition not only that different modes have different meaning-making potentials but also that the transformation of meaning through different modal agencies is a powerful catalyst for learning. This transformation or transmodalisation of meaning making through different modes, as defined by Newfield,[88] creates 'transmodal moments.' The simultaneous layering of modes, for instance, a combination of verbal, sensory and kinesthetic modes in a single transmodal moment of interaction, facilitates the transductive process of meaning making.[89] Furthermore, Newfield suggests that using a shifting set of semiotic tools, in this case modal agencies, facilitates the meaning-making process.[90] Transmodal moments (episodic activities) in semiotic chains create 'fixing nodes' for semantic design knowledge. Newfield refers to this as a dynamic process that produces moments of 'fixing' in the semiotic chain of learning or semiotic mode of realisation.[91]

During a singular transmodal moment, the multiple modes must be coherent configurations and these configurations must meet some basic criteria. Firstly, Murphy suggests that these modes must be perceivable in the moment of action and treated as meaningful.[92] Secondly, due to the fact that every student has their own preferred semiotic modes,[93] cognisance must be taken of the variety of different modal entry points (verbal/linguistic, logical/mathematical, musical, spatial, kinesthetic, intrapersonal, interpersonal and naturalistic) or, as Kress puts it, a complex ensemble of available resources.[94] These will act as motivational transformational forces through which the heightened enjoyment of the activities will trigger moments of learning.

Practical application and reflection

The context for the practical application of the framework was the Cape Peninsula University of Technology (CPUT), South Africa. The research was conducted during 2017 with the student cohort registered for the Foundation Programme in the Diploma in Landscape Architecture at CPUT (n = twenty-five).

A pre- and post-intervention evaluation of the design skill sets of each participant was conducted before and after the framework was implemented. The evaluation consisted of four parts: a pre-intervention survey, a design assignment, a Participatory Action and Learning (PAL) project, and an informal and unstructured interview. The pre-intervention survey indicated the intellectual disposition of each of the students in terms of their design skill sets in relation to the required design skill sets for students studying the programme. These results highlighted the contextual origins of poor design skill sets and how this weak foundation contributes to low design exposure and underpreparedness. The purpose of the design assignment was to evaluate the development of the participants' design skill sets and design knowledge transfer. The design assignments were assessed against the attributes of design ideas and design solutions. The PAL project consisted of a reflective drawing assignment and a verbal report on the drawing, recorded on video. The participants had to draw Venn diagrams using circles to represent the resources they used during their design process for the design assignment, and the sizes of the circles were indicative of the resource contribution to their design process.

This section provides a brief interpretation of the data and, more specifically, the data of three selected participants. The participant selection was implemented through a stratified sampling method. The design assignment results of the participants were used to group them into three subgroups: low (0.0–1.9 marks), medium (2.0–2.5 marks) and high (3.0–5.0 marks). Following the stratified sampling process, one participant from each subgroup was strategically selected as exemplars:[95]

- Low: Participant Twenty
- Medium: Participant Twenty-three
- High: Participant Twelve

Participant Twenty

Initially, Participant Twenty's level of creative self-efficacy was very low:

I am not an artistic person. I don't know anything about designs and stuff.[96]

Creative self-efficacy, as defined by Diliello, Houghton and Dawley, is a subjective belief in one's personal ability to be creative.[97] In Participant Twenty, this belief led to a perception of low creative capability and poor creative self-image judgment,[98] resulting in a resistance to engage in creative activities:[99]

So when I started the assignment my mind was blank.[100]

Diliello, Houghton and Dawley propose the concept of perceived organisational support (POS).[101] Individual creative behaviour is, according to Plucker, more likely to occur when a person perceives their learning environment to support creativity.[102] The design skill set modal agencies and, more specifically, the emotional modal agency seemed to have created a POS environment:

The first thing that helped me a lot outside was the peer groups because we were able to discuss it and as a group and everyone shares their opinion.[103]

In an authentic contextual teaching and learning environment, Participant Twenty was not only able to use her[104] physical and natural environment as a resource, but she also used it to bridge the gap between theoretical knowledge concepts and real-life application. She commented as follows:

> We had to look for examples of rhythms in nature and we [were] looking [at] trees and cars outside. So at least we had an idea of how our rhythm is.[105]

The sensory modal agency stimulated the following required sensory design skills: a sensitivity to natural features, topography and materials; a sensitivity to body movement and orientation; and a sensitivity to human scale.

Contrary to the participant's declared preference for the natural environment as a teaching and learning environment, she had a naturalistic intellectual disposition of only thirty-four percent, the second lowest of all eight intelligences. This is indicative that teaching to, for and through the intelligences exposed the participant to stimuli in areas not usually applied in classrooms which developed those low intelligence areas.

Participant Twenty-three

During the PAL project, Participant Twenty-three reflected that:

> Then I saw the word focus on the board, so I like sit and thought for myself and something that I learnt in class came to my mind and so I go, went up and did my idea.

This quote is indicative of the participant's spatial sensitivity to visual signs or representamen. These representamen facilitated the interpretational semiotic process of re-contextualising the theoretical concepts by means of a representational shift called analogical reasoning. Analogical reasoning, suggested by Goldschmidt and Smolkov,[106] is very important in the early stages of the design process, because the development of concepts and ideas during the early stages will influence the design decisions later. This can be seen in Participant Twenty-three's reflection:

> In the class the pictures helped me. Just reminds me of the approximate symmetry because it looks symmetrical but actually it's different. And the words [verbal analogy] twins and copy, it reminds me of a duplicate of something. Like everything has a duplicate. Remembering what we did yesterday because what we did yesterday helped me a lot because

of things I forgot but going back and just sitting still then the stuff flowed back in my mind so I could write it more easily.[107]

Analogical reasoning assisted Participant Twenty-three in the process of identifying and developing examples, related projects, scenarios and connecting experiences to solve design problems.[108] The implementation of the concept of teaching in the intelligences,[109] the logical modal agency, and specifically analogical reasoning enhanced the participant's logical design skill set.

The semiotic de-contextualisation process, an indirect representation semiotic tool that is part of the ideational modal agency, led to an indirect semiotisation process that re-contextualised the theoretical concept into a non-specific context so that it could be applied/represented in various contexts. According to the participant's observation, the semiotic transference between the theoretical concept and the context-specific icon was effective enough so that the participant could remember the context-specific icon and de-contextualise it into an abstract symbol:

> The drawing of the leaf reflection and the tree. First the leaf reflection [direct symbol] helped me just to see the mirror effect because I had to draw a pattern [abstract symbol] the other student have to redraw. And the tree, we had to do a asymmetrical drawing and a symmetrical drawing of a tree and that was very helpful because now I can see the difference between those two.[110]

Both the direct presentation and indirect representation semiotic tools (ideational modal agency) stimulated the following required skills of the participant's ideational design skill sets: ability to perceive the visual word accurately, ability to transform and modify initial perceptions via mental imagery, aesthetic cognition, ability to see the qualities of design and visualisation, and representation of concepts, ideas and spaces.

Participant Twenty-three remarked that the theoretical content course material semiotic tool, an ideational modal agency, extended the learning process beyond the classroom context and opened up more time for him to interpret the theoretical concepts:

> The notes helped me, because I can go through the notes by myself, step by step following easily. So I can understand it better than just going fastly through it.[111]

However, language barriers that some students faced hampered the effectiveness of the tool. Having to study in English, being a second or even third language for most students at CPUT,[112] reading and understanding the notes became problematic. Participant Twenty-three observed that both the theoretical content course material and the self-study semiotic tool were problematic:

> [T]he self-study and the notes, they didn't help me a lot because I studied, I went through them but I didn't understand it.[113]

Even though Participant Twenty-three struggled to understand the notes (ideational modal agency semiotic tool), as discussed in the previous paragraph, he noted that the physical action of drawing (sensory modal agency) in the notes supported the visual recollection process of the theoretical concepts:

> I love drawing and in the notes there was place for us to draw and that helped me a lot because we can see the things and draw it down so we can remember it.[114]

This co-implementation of the modal agencies not only facilitated the semiotic transference process but also strengthened some of the weaker semiotic links created by the other modal agencies. This concurs with Kress' notion that all modes enable cognition,[115] in particular the conscious use of synaesthesia, a translation or transduction between modes and senses, resulting in a pedagogy that incorporates multiple entry points for meaning making.[116] Gardner made a similar point: "If you want to teach something that's important, there's more than one way to teach it."[117]

Participant Twelve

During the post-intervention design assignment, Participant Twelve indicated that she was unable to understand and apply abstract symbols (a required logical design skill) and to use geometric shapes to re-contextualise an abstract symbol to an abstract interpretation:

> And then in class – but the shapes I didn't know what to do about the shapes.

However, due to the analogical reasoning method, a logical interpretation semiotic tool – the visual and verbal analogies – supported the re-contextualisation transference between the abstract symbol and the abstract interpretation and stimulated the recollection of the theoretical representamen:

I didn't know what to do about the shapes exactly until I read the verbal information and what helped me in the verbal information is the picture of the opposite twins and then I remembered what we did yesterday.

The participant observed her recollection of the theoretical representamen as follows:

[W]hat I remembered yesterday, it was the nature of how the sizes, the sizes of the trees and that's what made me remember of what to do on today's design, on the perspective one.

The theoretical representamen, an outcome of the logical iconic presentation semiotic tool, supported the semiotic transference between step four and step five (direct symbol to abstract symbol) of the modal agency meaning-making process:

[T]he sizes of the trees [to step five (abstract symbol to abstract interpretation)] made me remember of what to do on today's design, on the perspective one.

The modal agency meaning-making process structured the implementation of all three logical modal agency semiotic tools. It facilitated the meaning-making process through the constant transition, translation and transduction between different modes.[118] The logical modal agency stimulated the participant's skill to understand and apply abstract symbols in various contexts, identifying and using design precedents and understanding relationships between the whole and the parts.

Concluding remarks

Exposing the students to the different modalities, through the approach of teaching to, for and through their preferred skill sets, not only supported them to experience learning in ways they were most comfortable with but also challenged them to learn in other ways, thus enhancing their underdeveloped design skills. Multiple modal entry points shifted the attention away from underdeveloped skills as barriers to teaching and learning to engage the interest of students and facilitate the development of design skills of students with disparate abilities.

The implementation of the modal agency meaning-making process in an authentic, domain-specific environment facilitated the students' skills and knowledge development by bridging the gap between the understanding of theoretical knowledge concepts and the real-life application of those concepts. Extending learning beyond the physical architecture of space into a psychosocial, collaborative learning environment that encourages a diversity of approaches to identify and solve problems demonstrates that both skills acquisition and information processing reinforce and expand students' creative ability and perceptions.

Notes

1 Newton D'souza, "Revisiting a Vitruvian Preface: The Value of Multiple Skills in Contemporary Architectural Pedagogy," *Architectural Research Quarterly* 13, no. 2 (2009): 173–82, doi:10.1017/S1359135509990261.
2 Elisabete Cidre, "Using IPads as a Dynamic Learning Tool to Develop Skills in Graphic Communication and Enhance Spatial Awareness," in *First International Conference on the Use of IPads in Higher Education 2014*, ed. Nicos Souleles and Claire Pillar (Paphos, Cyprus: Simos Menardos Language Centre, 2014), 7–10.
3 Newton D'souza and Kinkini Chandrasekhara, "The Role of Design Skills in Design Review Conversations: An Analysis Using the Multiple Intelligence Framework," in *Design Thinking Research Symposium* (West Lafayette, IN: Purdue University: DTRS 10: Design Thinking Research Symposium, 2014), 1–22.
4 Cidre, "Using IPads."
5 Kathryn Moore, "Visual Thinking: Hidden Truth or Hidden Agenda?" *Journal of Visual Art Practice* 4, nos. 2+3 (2005): 177–95. doi:10.1386/jvap.4.2 and3.177/1.
6 Ebru Cubukcu and Gozde Eksioglu Cetintahra, "Does Analogical Reasoning with Visual Clues Affect Novice and Experienced Design Students' Creativity?" *Creativity Research Journal* 22, no. 3 (2010): 337–44, doi:10.1080/1040 0419.2010.504656.
7 Nigel Cross, *Designerly Ways of Knowing*, First Edition (London: Springer-Verlag, 2006), doi:10.1007/1-84628-301-9.
8 Gabriela Goldschmidt and Rachel Sebba, "Who Should Be a Designer? Controlling Admission into Schools of Architecture," *Architectural Research Quarterly* 4, no. 23 (2002): 1–22.
9 Hernan Casakin and Gabriela Goldschmidt, "Expertise and the Use of Visual Analogy: Implications for Design Education," *Design Studies* 20, no. 2 (1999): 153–75. doi:10.1016/S0142-694X(98)00032-5.
10 Nigel Cross, *Design Thinking: Understanding How Designers Think and Work* (London: Bloomsbury Visual Arts, 2019).
11 Bruce Cadle, "The Politics of Change, Craft and the Bauhaus Reborn: New Relationships in Design Education" (Graaff-Reinet, Eastern Cape, SA: Conference Proceedings of the Twelfth National Design Education Conference, 2009), 176–82.
12 Ibid.; Fathi Bashier, "Reflections on Architecture Design Education: The Integrated Design Paradigm," *International Journal of Science and Technology* 5, no. 1 (2016): 1–13; Nadia M. Viljoen, Ria Van Zyl and H. M. Van Zyl, "Design Thinking: Crossing Disciplinary Borders," (Graaff-Reinet, Eastern Cape, SA: 12th National Design Education Forum Conference Proceedings, 2009), 158–68.
13 Bryan Lawson, *How Designers Think: The Design Process Demystified*, Fourth Edition (Burlington: Architectural Press, 2005).

14 D'souza and Chandrasekhara, "The Role of Design Skills in Design Review Conversations."
15 Larry Rexton Barrow, "Cybernetic Architecture Process and Form: The Impact of Information Technology," PhD Thesis, Cambridge, MA: Harvard University, 2000.
16 D'souza, "Revisiting a Vitruvian."
17 D'souza and Chandrasekhara, "The Role of Design Skills in Design Review Conversations."
18 D'souza, "Revisiting a Vitruvian."
19 Rebecca E. Martin and Kevin N. Ochsner, "The Neuroscience of Emotion Regulation Development: Implications for Education," *Current Opinion in Behavioral Sciences* 10 (2016): 142–8, doi:10.1016/j.cobeha.2016.06.006.
20 Newton D'souza, "The Metaphor of an Ensemble: Architectural Design and Skill Convergence," *Journal of Design Research* 10, no. 3 (2012): 206, doi:10.1504/JDR.2012.047937.
21 Goldschmidt and Sebba, "Who Should Be a Designer?"
22 D'souza, "Revisiting a Vitruvian."
23 Woong Lim and Jonathan A. Plucker, "Creativity Through a Lens of Social Responsibility: Implicit Theories of Creativity with Korean Samples," *Journal of Creative Behavior* 35, no. 2 (2001): 115–30, doi:10.1002/j.2162-6057.2001.tb01225.x.
24 D'souza, "Revisiting a Vitruvian."
25 Ibid.
26 Sajjad Nazidizaji, Ana Tome, Francisco Regateiro and Ahmadreza Keshtkar Ghalati, "Narrative Ways of Architecture Education: A Case Study," *Procedia – Social and Behavioral Sciences* 197 (2015): 1640–6, doi:10.1016/j.sbspro.2015.07.213.
27 D'souza, "Revisiting a Vitruvian."
28 Bryan Lawson, "Schemata, Gambits and Precedent: Some Factors in Design Expertise," *Design Studies* 25, no. 5 (2004): 443–57, doi:10.1016/j.destud.2004.05.001.
29 Ibid.
30 Nico Botes and Zakkiya Khan, "In Your Hands and Self-Portrait: Introductory Spatial Design Exercises in the First-Year Studio," in *DEFSA Design Education Conference 2013*, ed. Susan Giloi and Herman Botes (City of Tshwane: DEFSA, 2017), 112–17.
31 Paula Wilcox, Sandra Winn and Marylynn Fyvie-Gauld, "'It Was Nothing to Do with the University, It Was Just the People': The Role of Social Support in the First-Year Experience of Higher Education," *Studies in Higher Education* 30, no. 6 (2005): 707–22, doi:10.1080/03075070500340036.
32 A. R. J. Briggs, J. Clark and I. Hall, "Building Bridges: Understanding Student Transition to University," *Quality in Higher Education* 18, no. 1 (2012): 3–21.
33 Finzi Saidi and Farieda Nazier, "Enhancing Learner Performance in Design Education for Disadvantaged Students: The Case of Diploma Programmes in Architecture and Jewellery Design and Manufacture" (Johannesburg, SA: Sixth International DEFSA Conference Proceedings, 2011), 183–91.
34 Briggs, Clark, and Hall, "Building Bridges."
35 Botes and Khan, "In Your Hands and Self-Portrait."
36 Aleksandra Gajda, Ronald A. Beghetto and Maciej Karwowski, "Exploring Creative Learning in the Classroom: A Multi-Method Approach," *Thinking Skills and Creativity* 24, no. 2 (2017): 250–67, doi:10.1016/j.tsc.2017.04.002.

37 Tony Herrington and Jan Herrington, *Authentic Learning Environments in Higher Education*, First Edition, ed. Amanda Appicello (Australia: Information Science Publishing, 2008), doi:10.1111/j.1467-8535.2008.00870_23.x.

38 Ibid.

39 Trudy C. Diliello, Jeffery D. Houghton and David Dawley, "Narrowing the Creativity Gap: The Moderating Effects of Perceived Support for Creativity," *The Journal of Psychology* 145, no. 3 (2011): 151–72.

40 Gajda, Beghetto and Karwowski, "Exploring Creative."

41 Jonathan A. Plucker, "Is Originality in the Eye of the Beholder? Comparison of Scoring Techniques in the Assessment of Divergent Thinking," *Journal of Creative Behavior* 45, no. 1 (2011): 1–22.

42 Ibid.

43 Diliello, Houghton and Dawley, "Narrowing the Creativity."

44 Johnmarshall Reeve, Hyungshim Jang, Dan Carrell, Soohyun Jeon and Jon Barch, "Enhancing Students' Engagement by Increasing Teachers' Autonomy Support," *Motivation and Emotion* 28, no. 2 (2004): 147–69, doi:10.1023/B:MOEM.0000032312.95499.6f.

45 Gajda, Beghetto and Karwowski, "Exploring Creative."

46 James M. Puckett and Hayne Waring Reese, *Mechanisms of Everyday Cognition* (Hillsdale, NJ: L. Erlbaum Associates, 1993).

47 Jason C. Cole, "The Construct of Creativity: Structural Model for Self-Reported Creativity Ratings," *Journal of Creative Behavior* 43, no. 2 (2009): 119–32.

48 Carl Bereiter, "How to Keep Thinking Skills from Going the Way of All Frills," *Educational Leadership* 42, no. 4 (1984): 75–7.

49 Janice A. Herrington, "Authentic Learning in Interactive Multimedia Environments," PhD Thesis, Perth, Australia: Edith Cowan University, 1997.

50 Lauren B. Resnick, "Learning in School and Out," *Educational Researcher* 16, no. 9 (1987): 13–20, doi:10.3102/0013189X029002004.

51 Allan Collins, John Seely Brown and Susan E. Newman, *Cognitive Apprenticeship: Teaching the Craft of Reading, Writing and Mathematics*, (Urbana-Champaign, IL: Center for the Study of Reading, University of Illinois, 1987).

52 Jeremy Roschelle and Stephanie D. Teasley, "The Construction of Shared Knowledge in Collaborative Problem Solving," in *Computer Supported Collaborative Learning*, ed. C. O'Malley (Berlin: Springer, 1995), 69–97, doi:10.1007/978-3-642-85098-1_5.

53 Jan Herrington and Thomas C. Reeves, "Using Design Principles to Improve Pedagogical Practice and Promote Student Engagement" (Hobart, Tasmania, Australia: International Conference on Innovation, Practice and Research in the Use of Educational Technologies in Tertiary Education, 2011), 594–601.

54 Sadhana Puntambekar, "Analyzing Collaborative Interactions: Divergence, Shared Understanding and Construction of Knowledge," *Computers and Education* 47, no. 3 (2006): 332–51, doi:10.1016/j.compedu.2004.10.012.

55 Mark Dudek, *Architecture for Schools: The New Learning Environments* (Abingdon: Routledge, 2000).

56 Rose Wiles, Jon Prosser, Anna Bagnoli, Andrew Clark, Katherine Davies, Sarah Anne Louise Holland and Emma Renold, "Visual Ethics: Ethical Issues in Visual Research," *ESRC National Centre for Research Methods Review* 11, no. 4 (2008): 1–43, doi:10.4135/9781446268278.

57 Nicholas Addison, Lesley Burgess, John Steers and Jane Trowel, *Understanding Art Education: Engaging Reflexively with Practice (Teaching School Subjects 11–19)*, First Edition (New York: Routledge, 2010).

58 Bob Jeffrey and Anna Craft, "Teaching Creatively and Teaching for Creativity: Distinctions and Relationships," *Educational Studies* 30, no. 1 (2004): 77–87; David Whitebread, Penny Coltman, Helen Jameson and Rachel Lander, "Guest Editorial: Play and Learning in Educational Settings," *Educational Child Psychology* 26, no. 2 (2016): 90; Philipp Alexander Freund and Heinz Holling, "Creativity in the Classroom: A Multilevel Analysis Investigating the Impact of Creativity and Reasoning Ability on GPA," *Creativity Research Journal* 20, no. 3 (2008): 309–18, doi:10.1080/10400410802278776.

59 Wiles et al., "Visual Ethics."

60 Hernan Casakin and Arjan van Timmeren, "Analogies as Creative Inspiration Sources in the Design Studio: The Teamwork," *Athens Journal of Architecture* 1, no. 1 (2015): 51–64; Cengiz Tavsan, Filiz Tavsan and Elif Sonmez, "Biomimicry in Architectural Design Education," *Procedia – Social and Behavioral Sciences* 182, no. 2 (2015): 489–96.

61 Diana P. Moreno, Alberto A. Hernández, Maria C. Yang, Kevin N. Otto, Katja Hölttä-Otto, Julie S. Linsey, Kristin L. Wood and Adriana Linden, "Fundamental Studies in Design-By-Analogy: A Focus on Domain-Knowledge Experts and Applications to Transactional Design," *Design Studies* 35, no. 3 (2014): 232–72.

62 Hernan P. Casakin and Gabriela Goldschmidt, "Reasoning by Visual Analogy in Design Problem-Solving: The Role of Guidance," *Environment and Planning B: Planning and Design* 27, no. 1 (2000): 105–19. doi:10.1068/b2565.

63 Gabriela Goldschmidt and Maria Smolkov, "Variances in the Impact of Visual Stimuli on Design Problem Solving Performance," *Design Studies* 27, no. 5 (2006): 549–69.

64 Casakin and van Timmeren, "Analogies as Creative Inspiration Sources in the Design Studio."

65 Jorge Pires, Manuel Pérez Cota, Álvaro Rocha and Ramiro Gonçalves, "Towards a New Approach of Learning: Learn by Thinking Extending the Paradigm Through Cognitive Learning and Artificial Intelligence Methods to Improve Special Education Needs," in *Developments and Advances in Intelligent Systems and Applications: Studies in Computational Intelligence*, vol. 718, ed. Á. Rocha and L. Reis (Cham, Switzerland: Springer International AG, 2018), 251–68, doi:10.1007/978-3-319-58965-7_18.

66 Hui Cai, Ellen Yi-Luen Do and Craig M. Zimring, "Extended Linkography and Distance Graph in Design Evaluation: An Empirical Study of the Dual Effects of Inspiration Sources in Creative Design," *Design Studies* 31, no. 2 (2010): 146–68. doi:10.1016/j.destud.2009.12.003.

67 Hernan Casakin, "Visual Analogy, Visual Displays, and the Nature of Design Problems: The Effect of Expertise," *Environment and Planning B: Planning and Design* 37, no. 1 (2010): 170–88.

68 Gabriela Goldschmidt and Anat Litan Sever, "Inspiring Design Ideas with Texts," *Design Studies* 32, no. 2 (2011): 139–55. doi:10.1016/j.destud.2010.09.006.

69 Casakin, "Visual Analogy."

70 Charles Sanders Peirce, *The Collected Papers of Charles Sanders Peirce, Volume 2: Elements of Logic*, ed. C. Hartshorne and P. Weiss (Cambridge, MA: Harvard University Press, 1932), doi:10.1038/135131a0.

71 David Plowright, *Using Mixed Methods: Frameworks for an Integrated Methodology* (London: SAGE, 2011).

72 Ibid.

73 Ibid.

74 Mihai Nadin, "Interface Design: A Semiotic Paradigm," *Semiotica* 69, no. 3 (1988): 269–302. doi:10.1515/semi.1988.69.3-4.269.
75 Bryan Lawson and Kees Dorst, *Design Expertise*, First Edition (New York: Taylor and Francis Group, 2009).
76 Brad Hokanson and Andrew Gibbons, *Design in Educational Technology: Design Thinking, Design Process, and the Design Studio*, First Edition, ed. M. Spector, M. Bishop, and D. Ifenthaler (London: Springer, 2014), doi:10.1007/978-3-319-00927-8.
77 Katja Thoring and Roland M. Mueller, "Knowledge Transfer in Design Education: A Framework of Criteria for Design" (paper presented at International Conference on Engineering and Product Design Education Artesis University College, Antwerp, Belgium, September 6–7, 2012); Bashier, "Reflections on Architecture Design Education."
78 Peirce, *The Collected*.
79 Casakin and Goldschmidt, "Expertise and the Use of Visual Analogy."
80 Pippa Stein, *Multimodal Pedagogies in Diverse Classrooms*, First Edition (New York: Routledge, 2007), doi:10.4324/9780203935804.
81 Howard Gardner, *The Unschooled Mind: How Children Think and How Schools Should Teach*, First Edition (New York: Basic Books, 2011).
82 Denise Newfield, "Multimodality and Children's Participation in Classrooms: Instances of Research," *Perspectives in Education* 29, no. 1 (2011): 27–35.
83 Ibid.
84 Gunther Kress and Staffan Selander, "Multimodal Design, Learning and Cultures of Recognition," *Internet and Higher Education* 15, no. 4 (2012): 265–8, doi:10.1016/j.iheduc.2011.12.003.
85 Newton D'souza and Mohammad Reza Dastmalchi, "Creativity on the Move: Exploring Little-c (p) and Big-C (p) Creative Events within a Multidisciplinary Design Team Process," *Design Studies* 46, no. 3 (2016): 6–37, doi:10.1016/j.destud.2016.07.003.
86 C. Nadia Seremetakis, "The Eye of the Other," *Journal of Modern Hellenism* 1, no. 1 (1985): 63–77.
87 Stein, *Multimodal Pedagogies*.
88 Denise Newfield, "Transmodal Semiosis in Classrooms: Case Studies from South Africa," PhD Thesis, London: University of London, 2009.
89 Zannie Bock, "Multimodality, Creativity and Children's Meaning-Making: Drawings, Writings, Imaginings," *Stellenbosch Papers in Linguistics Plus* 49, no. 1 (2016): 1–21. doi:10.5842/49-0-669; Pippa Stein, "Rethinking Resources in the ESL Classroom: Rethinking Resources: Multimodal Pedagogies in the ESL Classroom," *TESOL Quarterly* 34, no. 2 (2000): 333. doi:10.2307/3587958; Newfield, "Multimodality and Children's Participation in Classrooms."
90 Newfield, "Multimodality and Children's Participation in Classrooms."
91 Ibid.; Gunter Kress, *Before Writing: Rethinking the Paths to Literacy*, First Edition (Abingdon: Routledge, 1997).
92 Keith M. Murphy, "Transmodality and Temporality in Design Interactions," *Journal of Pragmatics* 44, no. 14 (2012): 1966–81, doi:10.1016/j.pragma.2012.08.013.
93 Gardner, *The Unschooled Mind*.
94 Kress, *Before Writing*.

95 L. R. Gay, Geoffrey E. Mills and Peter W. Airasian, *Educational Research: Competencies for Analysis and Applications* (Boston: Pearson Prentice Hall, 2012).
96 Quote from the pre-intervention, PAL recording.
97 Diliello, Houghton and Dawley, "Narrowing the Creativity."
98 Pamela Tierney and Steven M. Farmer, "Creative Self-Efficacy: Its Potential Antecedents and Relationship to Creative Performance," *Academy of Management Journal* 45, no. 6 (2002): 1137–48, doi:10.5465/3069429.
99 Ibid.; Diliello, Houghton and Dawley, "Narrowing the Creativity."
100 Quote from the pre-intervention, PAL recording.
101 Diliello, Houghton and Dawley, "Narrowing the Creativity."
102 Plucker, "Is Originality."
103 Quote from post-intervention, PAL recording.
104 The gender of Participant Twenty is unknown but the female form of pronouns will be used when referring to her.
105 Quote from post-intervention, PAL recording.
106 Goldschmidt and Smolkov, "Variances in."
107 Quote from post-intervention, PAL recording.
108 Goldschmidt and Smolkov, "Variances in."
109 Joan Hanafin, "Multiple Intelligences Theory, Action Research, and Teacher Professional Development: The Irish MI Project," *Australian Journal of Teacher Education* 39, no. 4 (2014): 126–41, doi:10.14221/ajte.2014v39n4.8.
110 Quote from post-intervention, PAL recording.
111 Ibid.
112 Eunice Ivala and Joseph Kioko, "Student Levels of Engagement in Learning: A Case Study of Cape Peninsula University of Technology (CPUT)," *Perspectives in Education* 31, no. 2 (2009): 123–34; M. K. Ralarala, E. A. Pineteh and Z. Mchiza, "A Case Study on the Language and Socio-Cultural Challenges Experienced by International Students Studying at Cape Peninsula University of Technology," *South African Journal of Higher Education* 30, no. 4 (2016): 231–55, doi:10.20853/30-4-572.
113 Quote from post-intervention, PAL recording.
114 Ibid.
115 Kress, *Before Writing.*
116 Stein, *Multimodal Pedagogies.*
117 Howard Gardner, "What Is Good in the Law and in Life," *The Professional Identity of Lawyers* 2, no. 3 (2016).
118 Kress, *Before Writing.*

Bibliography

Addison, Nicholas, Lesley Burgess, John Steers, and Jane Trowel. *Understanding Art Education: Engaging Reflexively with Practice (Teaching School Subjects 11–19)*. First Edition. New York: Routledge, 2010.

Barrow, Larry Rexton. "Cybernetic Architecture Process and Form: The Impact of Information Technology." PhD thesis, Cambridge, MA: Harvard University, 2000.

Bashier, Fathi. "Reflections on Architecture Design Education: The Integrated Design Paradigm." *International Journal of Science and Technology* 5, no. 1 (2016): 1–13. http://dx.doi.org/10.4314/stech.v5i1.1.

Bereiter, Carl. "How to Keep Thinking Skills from Going the Way of All Frills." *Educational Leadership* 42, no. 4 (1984): 75–7.

Bock, Zannie. "Multimodality, Creativity and Children's Meaning-Making: Drawings, Writings, Imaginings." *Stellenbosch Papers in Linguistics Plus* 49, no. 1 (2016): 1–21. doi:10.5842/49-0-669.

Botes, Nico, and Zakkiya Khan. "In Your Hands and Self-Portrait: Introductory Spatial Design Exercises in the First-Year Studio." In *DEFSA Design Education Conference 2013*, edited by Susan Giloi and Herman Botes, 112–17. City of Tshwane: DEFSA, 2017.

Briggs, A.R.J., J. Clark, and I. Hall. "Building Bridges: Understanding Student Transition to University." *Quality in Higher Education* 18, no. 1 (2012): 3–21. doi:10.1080/13538322.2011.614468.

Cadle, Bruce. "The Politics of Change, Craft and the Bauhaus Reborn: New Relationships in Design Education." Graaff-Reinet, Eastern Cape, SA: *Conference Proceedings of the Twelfth National Design Education Conference*, 2009, 176–82.

Cai, Hui, Ellen Yi-Luen Do, and Craig M. Zimring. "Extended Linkography and Distance Graph in Design Evaluation: An Empirical Study of the Dual Effects of Inspiration Sources in Creative Design." *Design Studies* 31, no. 2 (2010): 146–68. doi:10.1016/j.destud.2009.12.003.

Casakin, Hernan P. "Visual Analogy, Visual Displays, and the Nature of Design Problems: The Effect of Expertise." *Environment and Planning B: Planning and Design* 37, no. 1 (2010): 170–88. doi:10.1068/b35073.

Casakin, Hernan P., and Gabriela Goldschmidt. "Expertise and the Use of Visual Analogy: Implications for Design Education." *Design Studies* 20, no. 2 (1999): 153–75. doi:10.1016/S0142-694X(98)00032-5.

Casakin, Hernan P., and Gabriela Goldschmidt. "Reasoning by Visual Analogy in Design Problem-Solving: The Role of Guidance." *Environment and Planning B: Planning and Design* 27, no. 1 (2000): 105–19. doi:10.1068/b2565.

Casakin, Hernan P., and Arjan van Timmeren. "Analogies as Creative Inspiration Sources in the Design Studio: The Teamwork." *Athens Journal of Architecture* 1, no. 1 (2015): 51–64.

Cidre, Elisabete. "Using IPads as a Dynamic Learning Tool to Develop Skills in Graphic Communication and Enhance Spatial Awareness." In *First International Conference on the Use of IPads in Higher Education 2014*, edited by Nicos Souleles and Claire Pillar, 7–10. Paphos, Cyprus: Simos Menardos Language Centre, 2014.

Cole, Jason C. "The Construct of Creativity: Structural Model for Self-Reported Creativity Ratings." *Journal of Creative Behavior* 43, no. 2 (2009): 119–32.

Collins, Allan, John Seely Brown, and Susan E. Newman. *Cognitive Apprenticeship: Teaching the Craft of Reading, Writing and Mathematics*. Urbana-Champaign, IL: Center for the Study of Reading, University of Illinois, 1987.

Cross, Nigel. *Designerly Ways of Knowing*. First Edition. London: Springer-Verlag, 2006. doi:10.1007/1-84628-301-9.

Cross, Nigel. *Design Thinking: Understanding How Designers Think and Work*. London: Bloomsbury Visual Arts, 2019.

Cubukcu, Ebru, and Gozde Eksioglu Cetintahra. "Does Analogical Reasoning with Visual Clues Affect Novice and Experienced Design Students' Creativity?"

Creativity Research Journal 22, no. 3 (2010): 337–44. doi:10.1080/10400419.2 010.504656.

Diliello, Trudy C., Jeffery D. Houghton, and David Dawley. "Narrowing the Creativity Gap: The Moderating Effects of Perceived Support for Creativity." *The Journal of Psychology* 145, no. 3 (2011): 151–72.

D'souza, Newton. "Revisiting a Vitruvian Preface: The Value of Multiple Skills in Contemporary Architectural Pedagogy." *Architectural Research Quarterly* 13, no. 2 (2009): 173–82. doi:10.1017/S1359135509990261.

D'souza, Newton. "The Metaphor of an Ensemble: Architectural Design and Skill Convergence." *Journal of Design Research* 10, no. 3 (2012): 206–22. doi:10.1504/JDR.2012.047937.

D'souza, Newton, and Kinkini Chandrasekhara. "The Role of Design Skills in Design Review Conversations: An Analysis Using the Multiple Intelligence Framework." In *Design Thinking Research Symposium*, 1–22. West Lafayette, IN: Purdue University: DTRS 10, Design Thinking Research Symposium, 2014.

D'souza, Newton, and Mohammad Reza Dastmalchi. "Creativity on the Move: Exploring Little-c (p) and Big-C (p) Creative Events within a Multidisciplinary Design Team Process." *Design Studies* 46, no. 3 (2016): 6–37. doi:10.1016/j. destud.2016.07.003.

Dudek, Mark. *Architecture for Schools: The New Learning Environments*. Abingdon: Routledge, 2000.

Freund, Philipp Alexander, and Heinz Holling. "Creativity in the Classroom: A Multilevel Analysis Investigating the Impact of Creativity and Reasoning Ability on GPA." *Creativity Research Journal* 20, no. 3 (2008): 309–18. doi:10.1080/10400410802278776.

Gajda, Aleksandra, Ronald A. Beghetto, and Maciej Karwowski. "Exploring Creative Learning in the Classroom: A Multi-Method Approach." *Thinking Skills and Creativity* 24, no. 2 (2017): 250–67. doi:10.1016/j.tsc.2017.04.002.

Gardner, Howard. *The Unschooled Mind: How Children Think and How Schools Should Teach*. First Edition. New York: Basic Books, 2011.

Gardner, Howard. "What Is Good in the Law and in Life." *The Professional Identity of Lawyers* 2, no. 3 (2016).

Gay, L.R., Geoffrey E. Mills, and Peter W. Airasian. *Educational Research: Competencies for Analysis and Applications*. Boston: Pearson Prentice Hall, 2012.

Goldschmidt, Gabriela, and Rachel Sebba. "Who Should Be a Designer? Controlling Admission Into Schools of Architecture." *Architectural Research Quarterly* 4, no. 23 (2002): 1–22.

Goldschmidt, Gabriela, and Anat Litan Sever. "Inspiring Design Ideas with Texts." *Design Studies* 32, no. 2 (2011): 139–55. doi:10.1016/j.destud.2010.09.006.

Goldschmidt, Gabriela, and Maria Smolkov. "Variances in the Impact of Visual Stimuli on Design Problem Solving Performance." *Design Studies* 27, no. 5 (2006): 549–69. doi:10.1016/j.destud.2006.01.002.

Hanafin, Joan. "Multiple Intelligences Theory, Action Research, and Teacher Professional Development: The Irish MI Project." *Australian Journal of Teacher Education* 39, no. 4 (2014): 126–41. doi:10.14221/ajte.2014v39n4.8.

Herrington, Janice A. "Authentic Learning in Interactive Multimedia Environments." PhD thesis, Perth, Australia: Edith Cowan University, 1997.

Herrington, Janice A., and Thomas C. Reeves. "Using Design Principles to Improve Pedagogical Practice and Promote Student Engagement." Hobart, Tasmania, Australia: *International Conference on Innovation, Practice and Research in the Use of Educational Technologies in Tertiary Education*, 594–601, 2011.

Herrington, Tony, and Jan Herrington. *Authentic Learning Environments in Higher Education*. First Edition. Edited by Amanda Appicello. Australia: Information Science Publishing, 2008. doi:10.1111/j.1467-8535.2008.00870_23.x.

Hokanson, Brad, and Andrew Gibbons. *Design in Educational Technology: Design Thinking, Design Process, and the Design Studio*. First Edition. Edited by M. Spector, M. Bishop, and D. Ifenthaler. London: Springer, 2014. doi:10.1007/978-3-319-00927-8.

Ivala, Eunice, and Joseph Kioko. "Student Levels of Engagement in Learning: A Case Study of Cape Peninsula University of Technology (CPUT)." *Perspectives in Education* 31, no. 2 (2009): 123–34.

Jeffrey, Bob, and Anna Craft. "Teaching Creatively and Teaching for Creativity: Distinctions and Relationships." *Educational Studies* 30, no. 1 (2004): 77–87.

Kress, Gunter. *Before Writing: Rethinking the Paths to Literacy*. First Edition. Abingdon: Routledge, 1997.

Kress, Gunther, and Staffan Selander. "Multimodal Design, Learning and Cultures of Recognition." *Internet and Higher Education* 15, no. 4 (2012): 265–68. doi:10.1016/j.iheduc.2011.12.003.

Lawson, Bryan. *How Designers Think: The Design Process Demystified*. Fourth Edition. Burlington: Architectural Press, 2005.

Lawson, Bryan. "Schemata, Gambits and Precedent: Some Factors in Design Expertise." *Design Studies* 25, no. 5 (2004): 443–57. doi:10.1016/j.destud.2004.05.001.

Lawson, Bryan, and Kees Dorst. *Design Expertise*. First Edition. New York: Taylor and Francis Group, 2009.

Lim, Woong, and Jonathan A. Plucker. "Creativity Through a Lens of Social Responsibility: Implicit Theories of Creativity with Korean Samples." *Journal of Creative Behavior* 35, no. 2 (2001): 115–30. doi:10.1002/j.2162-6057.2001.tb01225.x.

Martin, Rebecca E., and Kevin N. Ochsner. "The Neuroscience of Emotion Regulation Development: Implications for Education." *Current Opinion in Behavioral Sciences* 10 (2016): 142–8. doi:10.1016/j.cobeha.2016.06.006.

Moore, Kathryn. "Visual Thinking: Hidden Truth or Hidden Agenda?" *Journal of Visual Art Practice* 4, no. 2+3 (2005): 177–95. doi:10.1386/jvap.4.2and3.177/1.

Moreno, Diana P., Alberto A. Hernández, Maria C. Yang, Kevin N. Otto, Katja Hölttä-Otto, Julie S. Linsey, Kristin L. Wood, and Adriana Linden. "Fundamental Studies in Design-By-Analogy: A Focus on Domain-Knowledge Experts and Applications to Transactional Design." *Design Studies* 35, no. 3 (2014): 232–72.

Murphy, Keith M. "Transmodality and Temporality in Design Interactions." *Journal of Pragmatics* 44, no. 14 (2012): 1966–81. doi:10.1016/j.pragma.2012.08.013.

Nadin, Mihai. "Interface Design: A Semiotic Paradigm." *Semiotica* 69, no. 3 (1988): 269–302. doi:10.1515/semi.1988.69.3-4.269.

Nazidizaji, Sajjad, Ana Tome, Francisco Regateiro, and Ahmadreza Keshtkar Ghalati. "Narrative Ways of Architecture Education: A Case Study." *Procedia: Social and Behavioral Sciences* 197 (2015): 1640–46. doi:10.1016/j.sbspro.2015.07.213.

Newfield, Denise. "Multimodality and Children's Participation in Classrooms: Instances of Research." *Perspectives in Education* 29, no. 1 (2011): 27–35.

Newfield, Denise. "Transmodal Semiosis in Classrooms: Case Studies from South Africa." PhD thesis, London: University of London, 2009.

Peirce, Charles Sanders. *The Collected Papers of Charles Sanders Peirce, Volume 2: Elements of Logic*. Edited by C. Hartshorne and P. Weiss. Cambridge, MA: Harvard University Press, 1932. doi:10.1038/135131a0.

Pires, Jorge, Manuel Pérez Cota, Álvaro Rocha, and Ramiro Gonçalves. "Towards a New Approach of Learning: Learn by Thinking Extending the Paradigm Through Cognitive Learning and Artificial Intelligence Methods to Improve Special Education Needs." In *Developments and Advances in Intelligent Systems and Applications: Studies in Computational Intelligence*, edited by Á. Rocha and L. Reis, Vol. 1, 251–68. US: Springer, 2018. doi:10.1007/978-3-319-58965-7_18.

Plowright, David. *Using Mixed Methods: Frameworks for an Integrated Methodology*. London: SAGE Publications, 2011.

Plucker, Jonathan A. "Is Originality in the Eye of the Beholder? Comparison of Scoring Techniques in the Assessment of Divergent Thinking." *Journal of Creative Behavior* 45, no. 1 (2011): 1–22.

Puckett, James M., and Hayne Waring Reese. *Mechanisms of Everyday Cognition*. Hillsdale, NJ: L. Erlbaum Associates, 1993.

Puntambekar, Sadhana. "Analyzing Collaborative Interactions: Divergence, Shared Understanding and Construction of Knowledge." *Computers and Education* 47, no. 3 (2006): 332–51. doi:10.1016/j.compedu.2004.10.012.

Ralarala, M.K., E.A. Pineteh, and Z. Mchiza. "A Case Study on the Language and Socio-Cultural Challenges Experienced by International Students Studying at Cape Peninsula University of Technology." *South African Journal of Higher Education* 30, no. 4 (2016): 231–55. doi:10.20853/30-4-572.

Reeve, Johnmarshall, Hyungshim Jang, Dan Carrell, Soohyun Jeon, and Jon Barch. "Enhancing Students' Engagement by Increasing Teachers' Autonomy Support." *Motivation and Emotion* 28, no. 2 (2004): 147–69. doi:10.1023/B:MOEM.0000032312.95499.6f.

Resnick, Lauren B. "Learning in School and Out." *Educational Researcher* 16, no. 9 (1987): 13–20. doi:10.3102/0013189X029002004.

Roschelle, Jeremy, and Stephanie D. Teasley. "The Construction of Shared Knowledge in Collaborative Problem Solving." In *Computer Supported Collaborative Learning*, edited by C. O'Malley, 69–97. Berlin: Springer, 1995. doi:10.1007/978-3-642-85098-1_5.

Saidi, Finzi, and Farieda Nazier. "Enhancing Learner Performance in Design Education for Disadvantaged Students: The Case of Diploma Programmes in Architecture and Jewellery Design and Manufacture." Johannesburg, SA: *Sixth International DEFSA Conference Proceedings*, 183–91, 2011.

Seremetakis, C. Nadia. "The Eye of the Other." *Journal of Modern Hellenism* 1, no. 1 (1985): 63–77.

Stein, Pippa. *Multimodal Pedagogies in Diverse Classrooms*. First Edition. New York: Routledge, 2007. doi:10.4324/9780203935804.

Stein, Pippa. "Rethinking Resources in the ESL Classroom: Rethinking Resources: Multimodal Pedagogies in the ESL Classroom." *TESOL Quarterly* 34, no. 2 (2000): 333. doi:10.2307/3587958.

Tavsan, Cengiz, Filiz Tavsan, and Elif Sonmez. "Biomimicry in Architectural Design Education." *Procedia: Social and Behavioral Sciences* 182, no. 2 (2015): 489–96. doi:10.1016/j.sbspro.2015.04.832.

Thoring, Katja, and Roland M. Mueller. "Knowledge Transfer in Design Education: A Framework of Criteria for Design." Paper presented at *International Conference on Engineering and Product Design Education*, Artesis University College, Antwerp, Belgium, September 6–7, 2012.

Tierney, Pamela, and Steven M. Farmer. "Creative Self-Efficacy: Its Potential Antecedents and Relationship to Creative Performance." *Academy of Management Journal* 45, no. 6 (2002): 1137–48. doi:10.5465/3069429.

Viljoen, Nadia M., Ria Van Zyl, and H.M. Van Zyl. "Design Thinking: Crossing Disciplinary Borders." Graaff-Reinet, Eastern Cape, SA: *12th National Design Education Forum Conference Proceedings*, 158–68, 2009.

Whitebread, David, Penny Coltman, Helen Jameson, and Rachel Lander. "Guest Editorial: Play and Learning in Educational Settings." *Educational Child Psychology* 26, no. 2 (2016): 90.

Wilcox, Paula, Sandra Winn, and Marylynn Fyvie-Gauld. "'It Was Nothing to Do with the University, It Was Just the People': The Role of Social Support in the First-Year Experience of Higher Education." *Studies in Higher Education* 30, no. 6 (2005): 707–22. doi:10.1080/03075070500340036.

Wiles, Rose, Jon Prosser, Anna Bagnoli, Andrew Clark, Katherine Davies, Sarah Anne Louise Holland, and Emma Renold. "Visual Ethics: Ethical Issues in Visual Research." *ESRC National Centre for Research Methods Review* 11, no. 4 (2008): 1–43. doi:10.4135/9781446268278.

2 Integrating critical and rhetorical writing in the beginning architecture studio

Andrew R. Tripp

Introduction

This chapter concerns the integration of writing in the first year of architectural design studio education. The topic of writing in the architecture studio is not new. Writing across the curriculum is generally associated with the educational movements of the early 1970s, which stressed critical thinking and collaborative learning. These movements survive today in the objectives of university-wide writing initiatives; nevertheless, these are typically championed by instructors outside the design studio and generally viewed as external and additional to the proper education of a designer, regardless of whether that education is defined as liberal or polytechnical. But what if this were otherwise? What if writing were taught by architects and viewed as foundational to their education? What would be the benefits and risks to students?

The purpose of this chapter is to assuage some of the doubts that surround integrating writing in the beginning architecture studio, to describe the benefits of such an initiative, and to provide some clear direction for developing courses with these benefits in mind.

Visualising the place of writing

For many students and teachers, the attraction to architecture and the so-called visual arts goes hand in hand with a repulsion from the language arts. With this in mind, it is helpful to begin with an image.

In the second decade of the seventeenth century, Pieter Brueghel the Younger painted a series of genre scenes depicting the interior of a village lawyer's office (1615–1621) (Figure 2.1). Over ninety versions of the scene exist, but only three exist as large-format wooden panels (roughly 75 × 125 cm). These larger versions differ from one another only in their colouration; they are otherwise identical in their composition and cast of characters. The popular description of these paintings suggests that they present "a satire on the venality of the legal profession and the way lawyers twist and distort the law."[1] Such an interpretation of the lawyer's ability to bend language to his will is appealing and would be entirely convincing were it not for the all-consuming and unforgiving avalanche of language represented by the written documents throughout the lawyer's office.

Written documents burst from satchels, hang from hooks, pour over the table and litter the floor. A missing windowpane is patched with a page. No single character in the scene can escape the written document. No single actor or agent – including the lawyer – is in a position to control or possess all of the writing; rather, writing takes possession of the characters themselves. It envelopes them topographically, variously protecting and exposing them. We are accustomed to observing figures grounded in the space of linear perspective, but here, in the banal depth of the village lawyer's office, the characters and their actions are grounded and set into relief by writing.

The lawyer is identifiable by his traditional headwear. He looks intently upon a document while the clerk, seated near the door, furiously transcribes the official record. The lawyer's gaze is preoccupied with his reading and the clerk's with his writing; engaged as they are with their letters, they are blind to the activities of everyday life unfolding in the centre of the room. A

Figure 2.1 Pieter Brueghel II Flanders, 1564/65–1637/38 *The tax-collector's office* c. 1615, Antwerp oil on wood panel 74.5 × 106.5 cm Bequest of Helen Austin Horn 1934 Art Gallery of South Australia, Adelaide 0.814

Source: Reproduced with the kind permission of the Art Gallery of South Australia.

half-dozen villagers have arrived with poultry and produce in hand to barter for the lawyer's services; their expressions range from anxious to angry. In the centre, a thin man with loose leggings – and morals, apparently – conceals his arm as he pilfers an egg from the woman bending over her basket. The would-be thief's misdirecting gaze is met by the glower of the upright young man beside the near edge of the lawyer's desk. At the opposite edge, a hunched figure whispers into the lawyer's ear and points at the document as if to indicate some minutiae that required legal attention. Concealed by this gesture, the whisperer offers the lawyer a small purse – a bribe – presumably to guarantee his advantage in the document's interpretation and the subsequent decision.

Each character is developed by their costume. The lawyer wears a close-fitting jerkin over a dark doublet and a white shirt. The older man in the centre wears the same costume, except that his hems have unraveled, which is to say that they are unfinished. These costumes are similar in the number and location of elements, but they differ in the degree of their finish. The young man's costume is more confounding. He wears a long pleated waistcoat over a white shirt and holds a richly lined jacket in his left arm. The progression from the jerkin to the jacket reflects the movement of fashion in the early decades of the seventeenth century.[2] On the one hand, the young man's outerwear reflects his attention to fashion and finish; on the other hand, his undershirt is uncharacteristically tight for this style of costume and there is a patch on its shoulder where a seam was recently repaired.

The art historian Emilie Gordenker has shown how the representation of costume in seventeenth-century Dutch portraiture paralleled the art of rhetoric.[3] The same is true for genre paintings. The choice of elements, as well as their arrangement and finish, was analogous to the invention, disposition and elocution of persuasive speech; furthermore, both dressing and speaking were thought to observe *decorum* by adapting to the circumstances of the time and place. In Brueghel's painting, *decorum* dictates that the two older men wear similar costumes, but the contrast in the degree of their finishing indicates their different stations within the same circumstances. The young man, on the other hand, is not aligned with either of these stations; the nature of his character as represented by his costume is mixed and indefinite.

This mixture is echoed in the young man's posture and spatial orientation. He faces the would-be thief, but his torso twists away from the villagers toward the lawyer and suborner. The young man embodies the "turning point" of the scene. He faces – and is faced by – a decision: whether to act against the thief in favour of the villager or to act against the bribe, which presumably would protect his own self-interest. Like his costume, his character is indefinite and depends on the choice between these competing orientations. His posture, commonly called *contrapposto* or *antithesis*, was understood at the time as a rhetorical figure that represented the artful balance of acting ethically, that is, acting upon one's knowledge of what should be said or done in difficult and changing circumstances.[4] Knowing what to say in a particular time and place is a rhetorical matter, but rhetoric in this context is also a model for ethics.[5]

Brueghel's painting is not only a satire on corruption in the legal profession, it is also a parable on – and for – the humanistic education of the young. The painting presents a visual form of a social imaginary in which the written word provokes ethical reflection in education.

Writing across the curriculum

The description of a painting – much like that discussed earlier – is a commonplace theme for writing in the design studio. In such an exercise, students are compelled to develop their observational skills through a close examination of a single visual artifact. This was the general reasoning behind an assignment written by the author that asked first-year undergraduate architecture students to describe the everyday settings and human actions represented in genre scenes ranging from Jan Steen, Pieter de Hooch and Nicolaes Maes to George Wesley Bellows, Edward Hopper and Julie Blackmon. The writing assignment was intended as a mechanism for assessing the students' learning and for improving their chances of retaining essential concepts; however, as one might expect, the students were unprepared for this kind of work. After sending several dozen students to the university's writing centre, the centre countered with a request for the instructors to participate in a quality enhancement plan for training educators in the best practices of integrating writing in traditionally non-writing-based courses. With the support of a grant through the provost's office, fourteen faculty members met every day for five weeks of faculty development. The specific outcome of this development was the renovation of a course that integrated writing across the curriculum: in this case, the renovation of the first semester of the undergraduate architecture studio sequence. Since its development, this course – including its basic outline, sequence of projects and documentation – has been delivered three times. A brief description of the renovated course is warranted.

Students enter the first semester of their architecture education from a wide range of preprofessional backgrounds, with a range of beliefs, interests and abilities. The goal is not to cull the numbers, but rather to prepare as many as possible for the challenges of the education to come. With this in mind, the new course is divided into five project-based learning modules with a progressively accumulating set of learning outcomes.

- Project One asks students to draw on their preprofessional knowledge of the everyday built environment to interrogate how and what architecture represents. It functions within the semester to prioritise observation, interpretation, iteration and critical thinking. Technical knowledge is subordinated, although the project covers basic spatial and geometrical skills through photography and cut-and-paste collage.
- Project Two concerns architectural polychromy. It functions to introduce intense and focused formal visual training alongside considerations of meaning and material. Working in acrylic paint demands a particular ethos, but it also supports an effective balance between increasing technical challenges and the immediate feedback inherent in reproducible visual effects. Most students entering their architectural education have very little experience with colour theory, and so the knowledge created by this project has the benefit of being new to all students despite the inequities of their socioeconomic backgrounds.
- Project Three takes up workshop techniques through intensive training in woodworking, metalworking and formworking (i.e., casting in plaster or concrete). Students gain knowledge of the standards they are capable of achieving as well as the process and patience required to continuously advance those standards. While this work is more explicitly technical, it concludes with assignments that require the integration of previous learning.
- Project Four is an exercise in synthesis, which means that it takes the first three modules and synthesises them in an open-ended problem-solving exercise. For the past several years, the problem has been to create an artifact that transforms a place of circulating into a place of residing. In more common parlance, students work in teams to create a chair sited on a stair (Figure 2.2).
- Project Five is reflective. It consists of a digital and hard-copy portfolio, generally formatted according to the student publication of the department or college (Figure 2.3).

In each of these projects, students are assessed in three major categories: products, processes and critical thinking. Products refers to the quality of their final artifacts and amounts to about half of the project grade. Processes refers to their attention to the phases leading up to the final artifact and amounts to a quarter of the project grade. The remaining quarter of the project grade is given over to critical thinking, which is where new

Figure 2.2 Krishna Desai and Olivia Baker, "Project 4: Dwelling Equipment,"
2016, red oak, approximately 16 × 24 × 24 in. (40.6 × 61.0 × 61.0 cm)

findings from the scholarship on writing across the curriculum enter into the course.

For each of the five projects, students are expected to accomplish a short writing assignment that is handed in along with their final product. This is typical, but far from the most important addition; more important are the short informal writing assignments the students accomplish by handing in their notebooks throughout the duration of each project. At the beginning of almost every class, students are given a two- or three-sentence "critical writing prompt" that asks them to explore and free-write about a particular topic or concept. Engaging in these exercises, which are spontaneous and last no more than fifteen minutes, prepares students for a lecture, discussion or presentation by providing a conceptual scaffolding that anticipates specific aspects of the upcoming learning experience; for example, a discussion on Gottfried Semper might be preceded by a prompt that includes vocabulary like "cladding" and "clothing." While informal, these exercises require focus and establish something like a ceremonial beginning for each class; then in hindsight, they provide a chronicle of the daily changes and challenges a student experiences.

It is important to note that these exercises are not aimed at improving the students' writing, but rather at promoting critical thinking and deepening their engagement with disciplinary specific subject matter. The major lesson of the university's faculty development workshop – a lesson that is well supported by research in teaching and learning – was that deep and engaged disciplinary learning through writing does not depend on the quantity of writing, but rather on the quality of the writing assignments. But what qualifies a writing assignment as good? Scholars are generally in agreement that a good assignment prompts a high level of critical thinking; initiates students into the big questions of a course; teaches disciplinary ways of making, observing, knowing, and so on; and promotes self-reflection or metacognition.[6] To enjoy the benefits of integrating writing, instructors must design writing assignments as they would design any project or programme, that is, with care. This is a daunting task, and it does not help that there are several widely held negative beliefs that discourage writing in courses like the architecture studio.

Misconceptions about writing in the architecture studio

The proposal to integrate writing into a beginning architectural studio is opposed by many misconceptions that are unrelated to the relative ease or difficulty of the actual teaching. Five of the most common misconceptions are considered and refuted here.

Misconception one: writing is not appropriate to an architecture course

Many of us believe that writing is appropriate in literature or history courses but not in an architecture studio. Certainly, writing has a place in the professional world, but the argument for its suitability in studio-based education is broader than professional preparation. What constitutes a writing assignment for a course is always up for debate, meaning that we are free to dismiss our preconceptions about what a writing assignment should look like. Writing can take almost any form from bathroom graffiti to dissertation to street signage and building wayfinding. Regardless of the assignment, writing is proven to challenge and condition critical thinking in students (Figure 2.3). Furthermore, it provides teachers with tangible evidence of that critical thinking, which is necessary if this is to be part of a formal method of assessment. For students, writing allows a direct opportunity to struggle with a specific concept or process from the discipline, or it may serve a metacognitive aim that helps students reflect on their own thinking and learning in the studio. Metacognitive strategies, including well-known strategies for reading comprehension and note-taking, are appropriate to any course in which students are asked to improve their ability to learn.[7] Students are remarkably open to the notion that there are specific techniques that have been proven to elevate their ability to learn.

Figure 2.3 Spurgeon Sanders, "Project 5: Magazine Spread," 2017, paper printout, 10 × 16 in. (25.4 × 40.6 cm)

Misconception two: writing will take time away from learning required content

Consider the difference between how much is covered or introduced by a teacher versus how much is learned by a student in a meaningful way. Then consider the rapidly increasing amount of knowledge associated with any given discipline, especially architecture. Robert Zemsky argues that educators should prioritise some contents over others and then teach the critical-thinking skills that will allow students to acquire and apply new disciplinary knowledge. Other research suggests that writing – especially reflective writing – can increase the amount of subject matter students learn by highlighting their learning as personal and purposeful and thereby motivate their learning outside of the classroom.[8] Writing in this sense can help a student identify and articulate the value of what they have learned for themselves and for others, which prompts deeper engagement with the content both inside and out of the boundaries of the classroom. Writing takes time, yes, but it also offers a depth of inquiry that quickens learning.

Misconception three: writing will bury teachers in grading

Adding writing to a course in which we are already attending to twenty hours of discussion each week sounds overwhelming, but keep in mind that research has shown that deep learning is not dependent on the amount of writing but on the quality of the writing assignments. There are many ways to provide quality writing assignments and reduce the amount of student work to be reviewed, graded or corrected. For example, many benefits of writing can be reaped by students even if the assignments are not graded, even if they are not read. In-class free-writing assignments – mentioned earlier – are an excellent way to scaffold key concepts and prepare students for class meetings. Spending the first fifteen minutes of class asking students to write in their notebooks takes nothing away from office hours and in fact improves the quality of discussion and the retention of content.

Misconception four: teaching writing requires special training or expertise to teach

Many of us believe that because we struggle with our own writing that we are not capable of teaching students how to write. Furthermore, as architectural designers, we do not know the intricacies of grammar, composition or the range of available genres. Research has shown that the best writing teachers are simply honest readers from within the discipline.[9] And there is good news about grammar: First, grammar is entirely a matter of *decorum*;

there is no universally correct grammar, there is only grammar that is appropriate to the circumstances of a particular time and place. Second, instruction in grammar and spelling has been shown to have minimal impact and diminishing returns on critical thinking; hence, in most circumstances we can ignore grammar.

Misconception five: students did not come to architecture school to be writers

No, it is likely that they did not; nevertheless, they are not granted amnesty from engaging the most significant concepts of our discipline. Integrating writing can improve a student's engagement with the subject matter of their discipline, which can improve the quality of their work as well as their sense of responsibility for it.

A method for adopting writing in the architecture studio

In his seminal book, *Engaging Ideas: The Professor's Guide to Integrating Writing, Critical Thinking, and Active Learning in the Classroom*, John Bean articulates an approach to course development with the intention of integrating writing for critical thinking and deep engagement with disciplinary subject matter. This approach, supplemented and tested with a review of the relevant scholarship of teaching and learning, provided the premises on which the earlier-mentioned first-semester architectural studio course was renovated to include writing. The following is a sequential summary of this approach for adoption in other courses.

Task one: embrace the general definitions and principles of critical thinking

Simply put, critical thinking involves "identifying and challenging assumptions and exploring alternative ways of thinking and acting."[10] "In critical thinking . . . assumptions are open to question, divergent views are aggressively sought, and the inquiry is not biased in favor of a particular outcome."[11] According to Richard Paul and Linda Elder, a "well-cultivated critical thinker" is characterised by their ability to "raise vital questions and problems . . . ; gather and assess relevant information . . . ; come to well-reasoned conclusions and solutions . . . ; think open-mindedly within alternative systems of thought . . . ; and communicate effectively with others in figuring out solutions to complex problems."[12] While there is agreement on the definition of critical thinking, there is little consensus on how it should be taught. One common approach, which is largely based on pragmatism, is to focus on the creation of arguments in response to open-ended problems. In this context, writing can be both a process and a product of critical thinking.[13]

Task two: organise the course to emphasise critical thinking as a cognitive learning outcome

Critical thinking is learnable. It is a practicable form of knowledge. In the renovated first-year architecture studio, the principle learning outcome is now for students "to demonstrate a basic ability to define, debate, and defend a project critically." Scholarship on teaching and learning has identified several principles for promoting critical thinking in course development. Central to these are the notions that assigned problems should motivate sustained inquiry, emphasise "applying" rather than "acquiring" knowledge, and require students to justify their work by including disciplinary appropriate evidence in their writing and speaking. Furthermore, courses that encourage collaborative learning and metacognitive strategies are shown to improve critical thinking in students.[14]

Task three: create a list of critical-thinking problems and prompts

Open-ended questions and problems that can sustain disciplinary and developmentally appropriate inquiry are not easy to generate amidst the normal strain of the semester. Bean suggests keeping a list of questions and prompts ranging from perennial issues to highly specific questions. Research in teaching and learning emphasises that a variety of modes, genres, and audiences promotes deeper and more meaningful learning.[15] Prompts created recently for the project on architectural polychromy range from an exercise in effective reading comprehension (i.e., previewing, preparing and paraphrasing)[16] to a reflection on the exercise of judgment throughout the various stages of the project to an imaginary presentation on polychromy to a room of practicing architects.

Task four: develop a repertoire of ways to deliver critical-thinking problems and prompts

Along with a variety of prompts, it is helpful to have a variety of ways in which these problems are presented or posed to students. These delivery mechanisms may include formal writing assignments; exploratory, low-stakes assignments; small group assignments; class starters, scaffolding, or free-writing assignments and questions; and practice exam questions. As mentioned earlier, group discussions in the first-semester architecture studio thrive when scaffolded by a variety of preparatory in-class writing prompts. When asked about the writing prompts in their end-of-semester course evaluations, students wrote "the critical thinking essays challenged my way of thinking and writing" and "the writings, in my opinion, were critical to each project because it gave us the opportunity to deeply reflect on what we were expected to learn."

Task five: create opportunities to include exploratory writing and talking

Kenneth Bruffee,[17] building on the work of Michael Oakeshott,[18] has shown how writing is entangled with conversation and partnership. The collaborative nature of conversation promotes the search for divergent views and alternatives and, hence, fosters critical inquiry. When this conversation is specific to our discipline, this critical inquiry points students toward the possibility of being experts in their field. One approach to this kind of conversation is to ask new students to write about how they imagine talking about architecture at the end of the semester, year, or degree programme. This gives them motivation to reflect critically on their existing knowledge while projecting or prefiguring their future selves: to partner and converse, as it were, with a possible version of their future self.

Task six: develop strategies for showing how our discipline uses evidence to support claims

Students are often baffled by the various types of evidence used by architects to support their claims. According to Bean, "Teachers can accelerate students' understanding of a field by designing assignments that teach disciplinary use of evidence or that help students analyze the thinking moves within an evidence-based argument."[19] Architects are particularly weak at acknowledging the circumstances of an argument and the need for appropriate kinds of evidence; nevertheless, there is value in paying attention to what vocabulary architects use to define, debate and defend their work as well as how this evidence changes depending on the time and place. Understanding when formalist evidence is appropriate requires understanding formalism in a meaningful and accessible way and, furthermore, in a way that distinguishes it from other approaches to architectural argumentation.

Task seven: develop a voice for coaching students in critical thinking

Aside from providing the opportunity for sustained inquiry, teachers need to develop strategies for nurturing, assessing and modeling the critical thinking and behaviour they imagine that their students should demonstrate.

Architects are widely familiar with the modes of coaching demands in a studio, but Bean also stresses that learning improves within a generally "supportive, open classroom that values the worth and dignity of students."[20]

Task eight: treat writing as a process

Writing can be both a product and a process of critical thinking; however, developing critical thinking takes time and practise, and the refinement of a final product can often truncate an opportunity for deeper engagement with a topic or concept (Box 2.1).

Box 2.1   "A student's reflection at the end of the semester," 2017

This is a collection of writings regarding our learning processes and project reflections over the course of the semester in ENDS 105. At first, I was unsure as to how these minor assignments were vital to my growth in studio, but as the semester went on I learned that jotting my thoughts down and then later forming them into coherent sentences solidified what I was learning in the studio. Regarding the project reflections, I gained a stronger understanding of what we learned and its significance, especially for the second project when we learned so much content in one month. It was helpful to sit down and reflect on each assignment and what I learned from it. I wouldn't say that my writing style improved, but how I explained the content definitely got better. I went from explaining the physical process of creating a good project to explaining the mental process of creating a good project (i.e., explaining how I got to the Big Idea, the Why, etc.), which is what really mattered.

Returning to rhetorical thinking

Our argument and method for the integration of writing in the beginning architecture studio has been largely premised on the link between writing and critical thinking. Provided that educators dispel their disbeliefs and misconceptions, it is not difficult to envision the benefits of challenging and conditioning critical thinking in the studio course. This argument for the value of critical thinking is abstractable and portable and thereby readily deployed in a range of discourse and debate from course and curriculum development to team teaching and recruitment. However, this argument also contains the thread of more aspirational objectives. Asking students to write in the studio provides a meaningful, practical and progressive manner of resisting the instrumentalisation of architecture and its education; it provides opportunity to practise eloquence, prudence and common sense in a way that is often marginalised by technical concerns. In this context, it is not only critical thinking that writing supports but also rhetorical thinking.

Recent scholarship on the importance of writing in teaching and learning has shown the importance of rhetorical thinking. Most disciplines, including architecture, construct their "interpretative community" with some reference to audiences, purposes and genres.[21] Of particular importance to our argument about the integration of writing is the notion of genre, which "refers to recurring types of writing identifiable by distinctive features of structure style, document design, approach to subject matter, or other markers."[22] The concept of genre can be confusing to students; however, it is readily explained by its analogy to clothing. Just as typical social occasions dictate typical kinds of costume, so too social occasions dictate conventional genres of writing with recognisable patterns, expectations and limitations. Genres are the framework of *decorum*; one asks whether something is appropriate to say, write or do within the framework of a genre. The rhetorical genres of a particular discipline "embody disciplinary ways of thinking and making knowledge,"[23] which also means they are a field of social action.[24] Genres assist in creating and disciplining the ways communities think and act; responding to a genre provides an opportunity to reflect on a social context as well as one's agency within it.

To quote Bean at length:

> Recent scholarship has shown that helping students situate their writing within a rhetorical context helps them transfer knowledge from one writing situation to another. . . . Because thinking rhetorically is such an important skill, writing theorists recommend that teachers build a rhetorical context into every writing assignment.[25]

Furthermore, a reflective awareness of genre promotes the transfer of learning between contexts; in other words, the transfer of learning between contexts is improved when genre differences are made explicit.[26] Thinking rhetorically, that is, conditionally and in terms of audience, purpose, and genre, hones the skills needed to transfer knowledge from one learning context to another.

Returning to Brueghel's painting, the final lesson is not whether the young man chooses correctly, but how his choice will give definition to his character – how it will form and reinforce habits that can be generalised and transposed from one social context to another. Integrating writing into the beginning architectural studio has been shown to offer deep and engaging disciplinary learning, but it is the opportunity to engage rhetorical thinking that offers a model for practising and generalising ethical knowing and acting. Contained within the relatively commonplace argument for critical thinking at the beginning of an architect's education, there is a much more precarious yet pressing argument for acknowledging and developing the link between rhetoric and ethics.

Notes

1 "Catalogue Note: Pieter Brueghel the Younger: The Village Lawyer's Office," *Sotheby's eCatalogue*, accessed September 14, 2019, www.sothebys.com/en/auctions/ecatalogue/2011/old-master-british-paintings-evening-l11033/lot.11.html.

2 Janet Arnold, *Patterns of Fashion 3: The Cut and Construction of Clothes for Men and Women 1560–1620* (London: Macmillan, 1985).

3 Emilie Gordenker, "The Rhetoric of Dress in Seventeenth-Century Dutch and Flemish Portraiture," *Journal of the Walters Art Gallery* 57 (1999): 87.

4 David Leatherbarrow, "Plastic Character, or How to Twist Morality with Plastics," *RES: Anthropology and Aesthetics* 21 (Spring 1992): 132; see also David Summers, "Contrapposto: Style and Meaning in Renaissance Art," *Art Bulletin* 59, no. 3 (September 1977).

5 Steven Mailloux, "On the Track of Phronesis," in *Disciplinary Identities: Rhetorical Paths of English, Speech, and Composition* (New York: MLA, 2006).

6 John C. Bean, *Engaging Ideas: The Professor's Guide to Integrating Writing, Critical Thinking, and Active Learning in the Classroom* (San Francisco: Jossey-Bass, 2011), 2.

7 Saundra Yancy McGuire and Stephanie McGuire, *Teach Students How to Learn: Strategies You Can Incorporate Into Any Course to Improve Student Metacognition, Study Skills, and Motivation* (Stirling, VA: Stylus, 2015).

8 Bean, *Engaging Ideas*, 11.

9 Ibid., 13.

10 Stephen Brookfield, *Developing Critical Thinkers: Challenging Adults to Explore Alternative Ways of Thinking and Acting* (San Francisco: Jossey-Bass, 1987), 71.

11 Joanne Gainen Kurfiss, "Critical Thinking: Theory, Research, Practice, and Possibilities," *ASHE-ERIC Higher Education Report* 2 (Washington, DC: ERIC Clearing-House, 1988), 2.

12 Richard Paul and Linda Elder, *Miniature Guide to Critical Thinking Concepts and Tools* (Dillon Beach, CA: Foundation for Critical Thinking Press, 2009), 2.

13 Bean, *Engaging Ideas*, 21.

14 Kurfiss, *Critical Thinking*, 88–9.

15 Bean, *Engaging Ideas*, 6.

16 McGuire and McGuire, *Teaching Students How to Learn*, 45–9.

17 Kenneth Bruffee, "Collaborative Learning and the 'Conversation of Mankind'," *College English* 46, no. 7 (November 1984): 635–52.

18 Michael Oakeshott, *The Voice of Poetry in the Conversation of Mankind* (London: Bowes and Bowes, 1959).

19 Bean, *Engaging Ideas*, 9.
20 Ibid., 10.
21 Stanley Fish, *Is There a Text in This Class? The Authority of Interpretive Communities* (Cambridge, MA: Harvard University Press, 1980), 14.
22 Bean, *Engaging Ideas*, 46–7.
23 Ibid., xii.
24 Carolyn Miller, "Genre as Social Action," *Quarterly Journal of Speech* 70 (1984): 152.
25 Bean, *Engaging Ideas*, 40.
26 Rebecca S. Nowacek, "Why Is Being Interdisciplinary So Very Hard to Do? Thoughts on the Perils and Promise of Interdisciplinary Pedagogy," *College Composition and Communication* 60, no. 3 (February 2009): 505.

Bibliography

Arnold, Janet. *Patterns of Fashion 3: The Cut and Construction of Clothes for Men and Women 1560–1620*. London: Macmillan, 1985.

Bean, John C. *Engaging Ideas: The Professor's Guide to Integrating Writing, Critical Thinking, and Active Learning in the Classroom*. San Francisco: Jossey-Bass, 2011.

Beaufort, Anne. *College Writing and Beyond: A New Framework for University Writing Instruction*. Logan, UT: Utah State University Press, 2007.

Brookfield, Stephen. *Developing Critical Thinkers: Challenging Adults to Explore Alternative Ways of Thinking and Acting*. San Francisco: Jossey-Bass, 1987.

Bruffee, Kenneth. "Collaborative Learning and the 'Conversation of Mankind'." *College English* 46, no. 7 (November, 1984): 635–52.

Carroll, Lee Ann. *Rehearsing New Roles: How College Students Develop as Writers*. Carbondale, IL: Southern Illinois University Press, 2002.

Carter, Michael. "Ways of Knowing, Doing, and Writing in the Disciplines." *College Composition and Communication* 58, no. 3 (2007). 385–418.

"Catalogue Note: Pieter Brueghel the Younger: The Village Lawyer's Office." *Sotheby eCatalogue*. Accessed September 14, 2019. www.sothebys.com/en/auctions/ecatalogue/2011/old-master-british-paintings-evening-l11033/lot.11.html.

Fish, Stanley. *Is There a Text in This Class? The Authority of Interpretive Communities*. Cambridge, MA: Harvard University Press, 1980.

Gordenker, Emilie. "The Rhetoric of Dress in Seventeenth-Century Dutch and Flemish Portraiture." *Journal of the Walters Art Gallery* 57 (1999): 87–104.

Kurfiss, Joanne Gainen. "Critical Thinking: Theory, Research, Practice, and Possibilities." In *ASHE-ERIC Higher Education Report 2*. Washington, DC: ERIC Clearing-House, 1988.

Leatherbarrow, David. "Plastic Character, or How to Twist Morality with Plastics." *RES: Anthropology and Aesthetics* 21 (Spring, 1992): 124–41.

Mailloux, Steven. "On the Track of Phronesis." In *Disciplinary Identities: Rhetorical Paths of English, Speech, and Composition*, 38–66. New York: MLA, 2006.

McGuire, Saundra Yancy, with Stephanie McGuire. *Teach Students How to Learn: Strategies You Can Incorporate Into Any Course to Improve Student Metacognition, Study Skills, and Motivation*. Stirling, VA: Stylus, 2015.

Miller, Carolyn. "Genre as Social Action." *Quarterly Journal of Speech* 70 (1984): 151–67.

Nowacek, Rebecca S. "Why Is Being Interdisciplinary So Very Hard to Do? Thoughts on the Perils and Promise of Interdisciplinary Pedagogy." *College Composition and Communication* 60, no. 3 (February, 2009): 493–516.

Oakeshott, Michael. *The Voice of Poetry in the Conversation of Mankind*. London: Bowes and Bowes, 1959.

Paul, Richard, and Linda Elder. *Miniature Guide to Critical Thinking Concepts and Tools*. Dillon Beach, CA: Foundation for Critical Thinking Press, 2009.

Summers, David. "Contrapposto: Style and Meaning in Renaissance Art." *Art Bulletin* 59, no. 3 (September, 1977): 336–61.

Tessmer, Martin, and Rita Richey. "The Role of Context in Learning and Instructional Design." *Educational Technology Research and Development* 45 (1997): 85–115.

3 Refocusing the interior lens

Other methods of critical and creative inquiry in the architecture studio

Anika van Aswegen

Introduction

This study explores and investigates other ways of creative and critical inquiry to enrich conventional design methods in the architecture studio. It introduces design actions not normally familiar in this context and that require students to adopt the perspective of the user as point of departure. A speculative workshop as descriptive case study[1] is used to conduct the empirical collection and analysis of qualitative data. It traces the journey of two students by representing their workshop narratives through primary data and observations by the researcher. The workshop, as disruptive 'plug-in', is introduced in an active design studio project, in order to investigate its influence on the design approach and attitudes of the students. The workshop is conducted in a third-year studio, the final year of undergraduate study. The investigation explores the usefulness of a human-centred approach, where the dynamic and fluid conditions of living are considered before providing physical architectural solutions. It aims to bring awareness of the contingent and temporal nature of people–environment interaction and people–people relationships within spatial design. It speculates that conventional methods of design alone are not supporting these fluid scenarios and that other ways of immersing the design student in complex design challenges could be instrumental in engaged learning. The objective is to uncover deeper design responses to prioritise users and real-life scenarios embedded in design projects, instead of the designer or architect's view and intent. In this way, the perspective of the 'interior lens' is adopted for design inquiry.

The workshop is the first in a series of four case studies forming part of a larger research project and sets the scene for the research to follow. Noteworthy observations are made regarding how students perceive and experience the intervention, how transformative learning is revealed, and what is learnt. Suggestions are made on how the process could be enhanced. The first investigation takes place within the interior architecture programme at the Department of Architecture, University of Pretoria. The department follows an ecosystemic approach[2] in which projects address interdisciplinary aspects amongst three spatial disciplines – interior architecture, architecture and landscape architecture. This educational context emphasises reference to architectural education, considering design reflection across different scales of human occupation in the built environment. This approach could also be referred to as spatial design education.[3]

Contextualising the theoretical background

The study is grounded in related architectural and design discourses and includes transformative education theory in order to contextualise the investigation. From the perspective of educational psychology, the focus falls on the ethical, affective and cognitive development of students. The effect of disruptive practice and the question of the potential value of empathy in transformative design inquiry are considered.

Agency, contingency and change

The promotion of change in architectural education and design pedagogy is not a new topic.[4] Literature, research studies and practice advocate for a paradigm shift from the "static domain-knowledge traditional approach" towards an "interactive dialogic approach"[5] that supports design research, or research-through-design.[6] If design pedagogy aims to bridge this gap, the question arises as to *how* this modified approach can be achieved. It requires a different mindset, one that not only focuses on student-centred learning but also includes real-life scenarios in the process. In addition, especially in the context of architecture and spatial design, a dialogic approach[7] therefore provides the opportunity to integrate the 'voice of the user' from the outset. The architect or designer therefore becomes a facilitator of the needs of others as an agent.

The 'better' definition of spatial agency, proposed by Awan, Schneider and Till in *Spatial Agency: Other Ways of Doing Architecture*,[8] outlines the role of the agent as "one who effects change through the *empowerment* of others, allowing them to engage in their spatial environments in ways previously unknown or unavailable to them, opening up new freedoms and potentials as a result of reconfigured social space."

As a consequence, the focus shifts from architectural aesthetics, style and building as object to acknowledging and actively engaging with the dynamic and temporal conditions associated with the occupation of spaces. The contingency of buildings and its reliance on the forces of uncertainty, use and change highlight architecture's dependence on external factors.[9] These are unpredictable and outside the control of the architect or designer and, in this context, the spatial agent engages "transformative intent" that is flexible and responsive[10] when dealing with complex design challenges. In this way, "architecture's dependency" becomes an opportunity for positive change, and the designer or architect assumes the role of a transformative agent as "citizen sense-maker" by letting go of preconceived perspectives.[11]

Adopting the user's perspective is an area in architecture for which a transformative shift is proposed. The idea of the architect as expert and problem solver in control of the design inquiry[12] is replaced by the user's spoken and unspoken needs and requirements as point of departure. The shift to the user perspective can be explained by shifting scales – from the scale of the building to people as the social scale.[13] When an architectural design is considered at 1:1, as compared to 1:100, the level of engagement with the human condition is revealed: "one has to confront the actuality of spatial occupation in all its mess and uncertainty."[14] In these conditions, the designer faces the changing requirements that shape the way we make meaning in the spaces we occupy. No recipe or library of parts can address the unpredictability of such living scenarios. In order to stay relevant, the designer needs to be equipped with ways of dealing with the unpredictability, while still allowing for the user's spatial agency.

This study argues that the user's relational interactions are integral to design inquiry. It informs decisions related to the agency of the user's occupation and appropriation of activities that are fluid and transient. The focus of a human-centred design approach then falls on situation-based priorities and not object-centred considerations,[15] In this way, the spatial design studio pedagogy reevaluates the unpredictable, temporal conditions embedded in design projects.

Agency in the design process

When traditional spatial design pedagogy struggles to support increasingly complex living situations, the conventional design process is also in need of review. Analysis, synthesis, appraisal and decision (with feedback loops in every design phase),[16] as a solution-led process,[17] is questioned for continued relevance, especially in a context where architectural drawings are seen as a "means of production . . . allowing the seamless translation from idea to architectural object."[18] If design education intends to increase its engagement and deepen the understanding of a human-centred approach, where users and not only clients are highlighted, increased immersion is needed in the design inquiry.

Through hybrid methods,[19] the user's voice can emerge through an exploration that represents time and the social, or "lived,"[20] nature of the built environment. This investigation proposes other design actions to extend the current familiar studio methods, because one mode of representation only considers one temporal condition.[21] Moreover, "[b]uildings and spaces are treated as part of a dynamic context of networks. The standard tools of aesthetics and making are insufficient to negotiate these networks on their own."[22]

Agency therefore relates to equipping the designer with engaged design actions with a human-centred approach, instead of striving for object-centred outcomes. This change in focus introduces empathy in the design inquiry, "to see the world through the eyes of others, understand the world through their experiences and feel the world through their emotions."[23] Human-centred design has received much attention, especially in industrial or product design,[24] and the discourse and practice of design thinking.[25] In design thinking discourse, many examples of human-centred design approaches start the process by immersing the designer in user experiences through an empathetic view. IDEO[26] and the UK Design Council[27] are two examples of establishments that follow a divergent-convergent sequence of design actions. The approach includes gaining a deepened understanding of the complexities of the requirements from the user's perspective, before the production phase commences.[28] These practices are widely prevalent in the industries related to social design and human-centred projects;[29] however, spatial design, or architectural education, needs to change focus in order to stay relevant.[30]

Conventional human-centred design has received much criticism[31] due to the perception that it is a quick replacement for detailed, qualitative social science research methods, which require time to obtain insight.[32] The fact that it is embedded as part of design thinking in business innovation,[33] to be used by anyone regardless of design background, draws further criticism of its rigour,[34] or lack thereof. Due to its emphasis on situation-prioritised human-centred design,[35] the case study furthermore acknowledges concerns regarding time and immersive engagement.

The deliberate insertion of a four-hour speculative workshop aims to determine how and where signs of transformative learning could be revealed. If the latter occurs, it shows potential for hybrid design methods to be assimilated in the traditional spatial design studio to extend and deepen the designer's understanding of complex design challenges. With understanding comes insight into the user's situation, experience, emotions and needs. Empathy assists the designer to shift the focus to a human-centred perspective.[36] Rival opinions regarding empathy include the danger of bias and selective application;[37] however, if affective and cognitive empathy is in balance, a well-rounded understanding emerges.[38] If people's experiences and needs are emphasised up front, the design process could reveal new possibilities for and attitudes towards the design of complex situations and real-life challenges.

Agency in the design process furthermore supports various actions to promote engagement. The 'think-make-share' model[39] as triangulated relationship provides an educational framework within which the human-centred approach can be explored: thinking while making, and sharing with peers. This model establishes the methodological underpinning for the ethical, affective and cognitive development of students in the design studio. In addition, the triad 'think-feel-do'[40] introduces 'feel', an affective quality that leans toward empathy and emotional concerns:

> This renewed way of thinking about design depends upon an equally reinvigorated concept of who the human being is. For too long we have simplified our world and thought of man in abstract terms, as if there were a single, universal human being who can serve as the common denominator for all of us. And for too long we have avoided delving seriously into the emotive, sensory, and phenomenological impacts of design.[41]

Introducing the intangible side of human requirements to design brings an unfamiliar focus into the architecture studio. This approach disrupts the conventional design inquiry and presents the possibility of positive change. Disruptive innovation has application in business management[42] and serves as a method to address complex social and environmental problems.[43] As such, it provides opportunities for creative inquiry and intervention in complex design challenges. The plug-in workshop becomes a disruptive action within the larger studio design project, aiming to facilitate change or transformation, albeit in a small way.

Educational developmental psychology

When a shift in design approach is required and students are expected to make cognitive, affective and ethical readjustments, educational developmental psychology contextualises the learning taking place. Many learning theories exist that relate to the development and growth of the individual, too many to include in this chapter. Due to the investigation's emphasis on immersive and embodied experiences, it relates to deeper human conditions. 'Ways of knowing' directly address 'connected' and 'separate' knowing as part of procedural knowledge.[44] Perry's scheme of development in college students[45] contextualises learning by focusing on cognitive and ethical considerations in development by proposing different stages: (i) dualism, (ii) multiplicity, (iii) contextual relativism and (iv) commitment. These form a developmental line along which students grow.

When these theories are considered, qualitative data analysis reveals that third-year students participating in this workshop are positioned on a threshold in their development. The transition between Perry's 'multiplicity' (diverse views and multiple perspectives), 'contextual relativism' (qualitative and contextual with evidence) and 'commitment' (ethical rather than cognitive development)[46] explains the growth and the challenges students experience in this process. The research study in *Women's Way of Knowing*[47] extends Perry's investigation holistically by considering voice, mind and self as ways of knowing. The perspective of procedural knowing focuses on 'connected knowing' that is "grounded in empathy and care" instead of separate knowledge, which is associated with reason and critical thinking.[48] Mezirow's 'frames of reference'[49] highlight the importance of personal beliefs, opinions and judgements. The question concerning the degree to which these fundamental aspects can be challenged remains unanswered at this point, also within the larger context of the investigation.

This chapter draws on the relation between 'contextual relativism'[50], where students give meaning to the embodied experience of the site and context, as well as on the disruptive process in the studio that has the potential to influence the larger design project in some way. In addition, when the designer asserts the perspective of the user by adopting a human-centred view, 'connected knowing'[51] enables deeper understanding and insight in design contexts where design challenges are sometimes difficult to articulate or frame.

Methodology and the 'plug-in'

The social constructivist paradigm[52] supports this qualitative study, in which students are active participants by deriving meaning from the design activities taking place in the workshop. During the in situ investigation in the design studio, the researcher and research assistant observe and document the real-life milieu of and activities in the workshop. This process provides the opportunity for triangulation[53] amongst the primary data collected, the activities of students recorded during the workshop, the researcher's field and reflexive notes and photographic documentation, and the research assistant's field notes. An inductive approach[54] is followed, in which observations and qualitative data analysis inform preliminary findings that are synthesised in related theory.

The workshop follows an instrumental case study design, where the emphasis falls on the issue of investigation and not on the case itself.[55] This is deliberate to contextualise the exploration in a larger sample at a later stage. However, reporting on the preliminary findings is noteworthy, as it provides an opportunity to speculate about the impact of the disruptive practice. Since the aim with the workshop is not to create a tool or model for use, it is important to extend the discourse of design research or research-through-design[56] as a stimulus for engaged learning. The observations made by the researcher and research assistant are as integral to the data analysis as the creative output of students is during the workshop. The study complies with the full research ethics approval that supports this investigation. In addition, all students grant informed consent for participation in the workshop.

The speculative workshop

This study reports on the first of four workshops that form part of a larger research project. The workshop introduces other ways of design engagement in an active studio project, with the aim of expanding design complexity and richness within a traditional design context. Furthermore, it prioritises the complex needs and experiences of users and embeds that in the framing of the project.[57] The insertion or disruption challenges the current *status quo* of design methodology in the spatial design studio. The objective is to determine whether students can adopt a different perspective – the opinion of the user rather than the designer – to assume a human-centred approach. The disruption can be considered deliberate or critical: inserting unexpected activities to foster other perspectives and attitudes during the conventional process.

This idea of disruption in this workshop forms part of a speculative inquiry that does not attempt to give solutions like other established disruptive design methods.[58] Nor does it aim to replace conventional design practices, as is the case with disruptive innovation in business, where existing markets and networks are displaced.[59] The primary goal is to unsettle familiar practices and to focus awareness on relational encounters between people in contexts and situations that are fluid and changing. The hybrid methods workshop is inserted as a disruption into a corporate office design project for a third-year interior architecture studio. The studio design project is partly interdisciplinary, with students from the three spatial design programmes collaborating in groups. They first develop an urban strategy and block vision for the selected part of the city. The corporate workplace design project is framed by this context and students propose a client, informed by the contextual understanding obtained during the first two weeks of the project. The project focuses on agile workplace design considerations within this context, but using a virtual building as site. Consequently, students need to imagine and visualise the immediate 'virtual' environment after their embodied experience of the city.

The workshop includes a series of activities to elicit immersive and connected ways of engagement. This collection of activities contains a selection of examples only and does not represent an exhaustive array of possible design actions. As a plug-in intervention, it introduces ways of engagement that are not normally associated with an architectural design studio.

Activities to provoke a different way of thinking

A four-hour series of activities upsets the familiar practice but also supports the larger design project with the purpose of deepening the richness and understanding of the complex design matters. By introducing a different lens, that is, a human-centred approach, students are required to recall their embodied experiences of the inner city – the site of the design project – as firsthand experiences. In this way, they immerse themselves in a different understanding of the realities of the city, its challenges and the issues people deal with daily. By critically reflecting on this immersion, their direct experience introduces a connection to the city and its users in a deeper way.

The workshop activities are intended to engage these experiences, activating various modes of engagement: problem statement, descriptive keywords, spontaneous vignettes and critical artefacts, with the inclusion of peer and self-reflection and a reflective essay. The work of two students demonstrates the modes of design inquiry and the subsequent engagement, from beginning to end. The narratives of their journeys articulate their critical reflections[60] during the process by documenting the trajectory of engagement. The value of the workshop in the context of the larger studio project reveals the nature of transformative learning.

Problem statements

Problem statements are personal descriptions of issues students identify in the context, perceived while on the immersive walkabout of the city. Noteworthy in the students' statements is the connection or detachment with which they reflect on their experience by expressing in first- or third-person voices. Student One observes objectively and reports on what is amiss and then proposes how this can be rectified: "In the city, there is a severe lack of public space and public event [sic] there is a barrier between the streets and the claimed 'open-to-public' spaces . . . BUT when people start to play music or sing . . ." (Student One). Student Two takes a different approach; her description is very personal and related in the first person:

> I live in the city, but I am not part of it. I have a story like everyone in the city but nobody to share it with. We are all different but similar in a

way, yet we are disconnected. I wish (to tell my journey) to belong and to be part of the city (Student Two).

These two accounts show two very different ways in which the same context can be experienced, depending on a person's point of view. After a new experience, the first student expresses potential, while the second student, intimately familiar with the city, feels like an outsider.

Descriptive keywords

Descriptive keywords (Figure 3.1), informed by the problem statements, are used as enablers to activate the students' thinking process. Instead of nouns describing static objects, abstract nouns, adverbs and adjectives highlight the abstract, dynamic and transient conditions of the city, introducing a different understanding of the problems, challenges and opportunities of the changing and impermanent aspects of the environment in which architecture exists.

Student One responds with keywords expressing hope and possibility through an imagined spirit of the inner city: "articulating", "heartfelt", "inspired", "harmony", "radiating", "resilience", "transcending", "echoes", "fading", "ascending", "articulating" and "inspired." In this way, the latent potential of the inner city is articulated by reflecting on socioeconomic challenges. The prospect of music as connector and community enabler is proposed to increase human interaction within the context of the workplace design project. The way the words are arranged, intersecting and forming a network, supports this observation. Student Two uses words of a positive nature, compared to the problem statement: "communication", "spirit", "connection", "character", "sharing", "culture", "beauty", "history" and "belonging." Only two of the words express a personal experience of "loneliness" and "fear". In both cases, keywords describe experiences, opportunities and delights. Student Two uses critical reflection to reevaluate the words and adjusts according to her immersive response.

Spontaneous vignettes

Spontaneous vignettes (Figure 3.2) become a link between thinking and making, as students visualise the issues they observe and experience. Keywords are translated into a collection of vignettes or impressions by the students imagining themselves as users in the city. Student One represents the drama of experience and vibrant interactions on the sidewalk. Her exploratory drawings emphasise the relational and connective matters over object and form-based inquiries, where static and physical structures become the backdrop

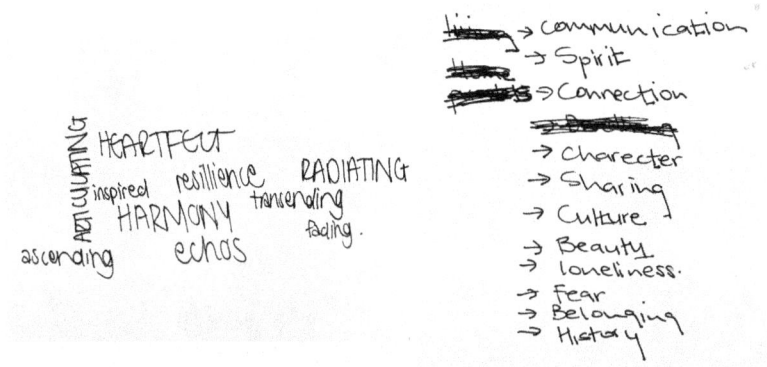

Figure 3.1 Descriptive keywords (Student One, left; Student Two, right)

to dynamic human interactions. The vignettes have an emotive quality and contextualise the relation between the people–people and people–spatial relationships.

Student Two takes a multi-scalar approach by zooming out to demonstrate feelings of fear, intimidation and anxiety on an urban scale, in an environment that does not support informal activities. Then, by zooming in on the micro, human relations become visible as vendors sell goods. The interaction between people is noted; however, one of the annotations refers to the "disconnection between the city and its people" (Student Two). In this light, commentary is given on the lack of spatial agency and opportunities for fluid and changing scenarios to develop.

Critical artefacts

The making of critical artefacts (Figure 3.3) requires students to look beyond objects, products, spaces and buildings and to express in abstract terms the issues of concern in order to evoke a different design awareness and attitude. A material library of 'second-life objects' is used to challenge students to go beyond conventional responses. When they consider objects with prior meaning inscribed by their former use, opportunities for deeper interpretations and abstract associations become possible, which would not have been the case with the use of conventional model-building materials, scale rulers and cutting mats. Preconceived notions are therefore tested in the process of 'thinking while making'.

Strong symbolism and abstraction can be observed in both students' critical artefacts; however, each interpretation has a different focus.

Figure 3.2 Spontaneous vignettes (Student One, left; Student Two, right)

Student One considers the concept of ascension (interpreted as freedom) as inclusive of everyone. Natural and manmade materials are integrated, strengthening the sense of belonging in the community (people in relation to each other) and in the built environment. Natural plant materials are appropriated from the university gardens to represent the temporal and changing character of social and fluid interaction. In the critical reflection, special mention is made of the presence of everyday rituals embedded in social interactions. The student's written reflection further shows that "this object is a compilation of various materials that come together in a quite unconventional harmony. There are elements in the composition that will change over time, contributing to the temporal 'being' reflected in cities".

Student Two expresses reflective thought in the making of the artefact. She mentions that, at first, consideration of materials was not specific, but in the making process, meaning was assigned to objects specifically. "This also helped me to start viewing the model with meaning and making it more personal. The model symbolises how all the people in the city are different but there is a similar golden thread that connects all of them even though it is not visible [at] first" (Student Two).

The critical artefacts reveal a deeper connection to the issues students identify during the process. They internalise matters more intensely. Meaning making and symbolism, because of associations with second-life objects, are two noteworthy aspects that assist students in the translation and representation of complex matters. The emphasis therefore shifts to understanding, instead of creating a conventional model. It unlocks active discussion amongst them, addressing the different perspectives and interpretations that the students express.

Critical peer reflection

During the workshop, students share with peers to get different opinions and inputs that could lead to other insights and extend current views. Interaction is important for cognitive, affective and ethical development, as students connect with one another as part of the learning process and, in addition, challenge their own preconceived views.

Peer feedback reflecting on the work of Student One supports the link between the initial keywords and the interpretation of the critical artefact. "The relationship between the position statement and the model is well expressed and fully ties in to the concept of creating events [in] an existing 'eventless' space" (Student Three). Once the student adopts the perspective of the user, immersion in the contextual understanding increases and the student imagines an atmosphere where "overlapping programs/daily rituals and essence" become the radiating power in the city as "one communal activity: music (in whatever form it may take)" (Student One).

Comments regarding the work of Student Two detail the lack of community in the current city context and appreciate suggestions to alleviate the issues. The students show a critical voice and discernment in the understanding of not only their own work but also each other's.

The reflective essay

A written self-reflection reveals experiences in three areas: (i) the introduction of hybrid methods in the studio, (ii) the adoption of a user perspective and (iii) the use of second-life objects and materials.

The different modes of engagement facilitate a deepening of insight into matters that students identified at the start of the workshop. The first student emphasises a conceptual approach and understanding, by taking into consideration a scenario-based human-centred approach. She highlights temporality and time, together with fluid relationships associated with event and interaction. The final observation in the critical reflection states: "The aim however is not to formalise the 'singing in the streets', but merely to extend it. Extending the delight from street to urban block, to urban interior and into interior interaction and experience" (Student One). A multi-scalar understanding of human needs at different levels and points of intersection are expressed.

Student Two takes the reflective essay very personally by considering her knowledge of and connection to the city. She expresses, again in first person: "The workshop helped me reflect on how I know the city, not only

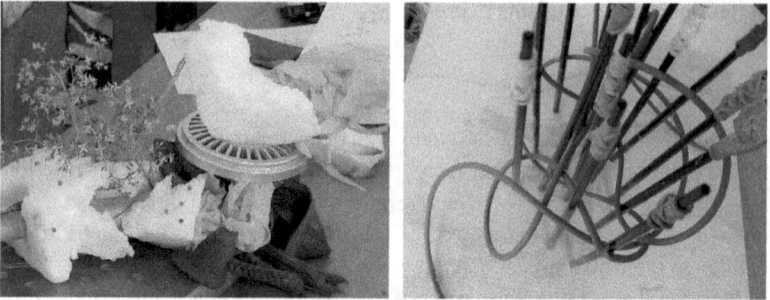

Figure 3.3 Critical artefacts (Student One, left; Student Two, right)

as a user but also as a spectator viewing the city from the outside" (Student Two). She demonstrates awareness of her perspective and inverts the connected-separate view, because she lives in the city as an 'insider'. As such, taking an 'outsider' perspective reveals issues in a different way: "The city is our home even if it is temporary" (Student Two).

Qualitative content analysis

The study is supported by qualitative data analysis without coding.[61] This chapter reports on initial findings derived from primary data collected in the speculative workshop. The identification of "keywords in context"[62] as a method for data analysis reveals preliminary concepts. These concepts relate to the meanings students assign to aspects of the workshop interaction to demonstrate their approach to human-centredness. The phrases the students use to express their interpretation and opinions provide insight into their relatedness to the workshop activities. In addition, it reveals their understanding of design challenges, with particular emphasis on human-centredness and situational priorities.[63]

Table 3.1 outlines selected examples of keywords in context and positions these (with phrases, emphasis added) in the left column; the context of use is given in the middle column (where meaning is assigned); and the right column contains the concept. The table highlights some of the complex considerations students reveal in their work.

From this analysis, design values related to human-centredness can be observed: spatial agency, dynamic and temporal conditions of living, meaning making and connected learning are expressed. With assimilation of these design values, the conventional approach in architecture which emphasises building can be extended to deliberately acknowledge the social over the

Table 3.1 Keywords in context

Concept: Human-Centredness

KEYWORD in phrase	CONTEXT of meaning	CONCEPT
The aim however is not to formalise the "singing in the streets", but merely to extend it (Student One)	Facilitate change and appropriation Supplement, add to richness	**ENABLING** [responsive, relational]
The city is our home even if it is temporary (Student Two)	A place to belong and be safe Connections	**BELONGING** [emotional connection]
[A]nd how each people group exists as something more when enfolded together (Student Four)	Relationships Collective enrichment through interwoven cultures	**COMMUNITY** [representative, identity]
The items on sale are representative of people in the city (Student Five)	Association with objects Symbolism and message	**MEANING** [physical, emotional]
[A]s you start focusing on the people and how they use the space, you start to realise how important human interaction is (Student Six)	Interface between people and objects/spaces Relational encounters and use	**INTERACTION** [interface, behavioural patterns]
[S]ee the city in a different light and (also) getting to see the growth and potential it holds starting from the bottom up (Student Seven)	Diversity and change Respect, acceptance of different perceptions/ views	**INCLUSION** [attitude, potential]
This brings the emotive feel of a space out into the open. How the user experiences the movement from their entrance to their destination until their exit again (Student Eight)	Emotive qualities of spaces Journey of user moving through spaces	**EXPERIENCE** [message, intent]

formal, thus acknowledging the unpredictable conditions and interactions outside the control of the designer or architect, which are often sidelined in the design process. Under each value, an associated concept lists possible considerations for design inquiry. Table 3.1 is not an exhaustive representation of possible considerations, nor is it an attempt to create a model or framework for human-centred design values. Figure 3.4 indicates the relational links which emphasise the fluidity and open interpretation that human-centred design values provide. The findings only report on noteworthy observations that highlight other ways of engagement – immersive

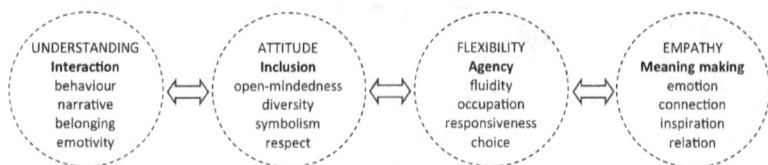

Figure 3.4 Human-centred values

ways. Further research is required to contextualise the initial findings by completing the full spectrum of the case studies envisaged for the larger research project.

Early observations

The preliminary findings report on the potential for transformative learning in the context of the plug-in workshop as a 'snapshot' of the first case study. Early observations reveal points emerging from the qualitative data analysis. These relate to human-centredness, agency and contingency, as well as ways of engagement and transformative learning. The theoretical background supports the investigation. In addition, the discussion includes matters that could not be foreseen at the start of the workshop as part of the inductive approach and also addresses the questions of empathy and of sustaining small shifts and the impact of disruption.

Human-centredness, agency and contingency

Initial findings show that the disruption has an effect on how students engage with the design inquiry during the workshop. It unsettles their conventional ways of working, but soon enables and activates unforeseen responses – such as connected design engagement. The workshop assists students to adopt different perspectives, not only prioritising the view of the user but also acknowledging opinions by peers. It is as yet unclear how a refocused approach can be taken forward and how it could be internalised as part of a new praxis in the future. Observations show that some students immerse themselves in the city and its people by documenting experiences in the first person, 'a connected voice',[64] as a daily user of the city. Other students are able to identify pressing matters in discussions with peers that would otherwise be missed without a human-centred lens, but documenting it in a 'separate'[65] or third-person voice. As a result of the disruptive nature of the workshop, students express their personal experiences in terms of emotional connotations. Due to the immersive approach, uncertainty and hesitation at the start are replaced by excitement and an eager participation during the course of the activities, especially in the making of the critical artefact.

Students who remain connected demonstrate another understanding in design, one that neither is prescriptive nor aims to control. Instead, this approach effectively enables choice and appropriation by the user by expanding the existing, rather than formalising the activities in some way. It demonstrates the students' awareness of a human need to perform certain activities spontaneously and the fact that not everything can be controlled through design.[66] This approach empowers the user and modifies the conditions of the project for the designer. Data reveal students expressing design intent, which can enable interaction and connection between people and which is fluid and temporal. Two-thirds of the class is represented in this group.

The rest of the students reveal evidence of an understanding of site and context that now includes the experiential, albeit in a disconnected way. Verbs, as action words, are used to relate the spontaneous vignettes as visual representations of the experiences of the user. Descriptions, textual and visual, add another layer of complexity to the understanding of the existing conditions in the city. Associations are extended further in the making process, where connections between second-life materials and abstract concepts represent complex social and contextual challenges. Through discourse and peer interaction, new meanings are found. These focus on community, inclusion, equal opportunities and finding a place, a home, in the city. Temporality and fluid relationships are two concepts emerging from the use of hybrid methods. The findings show that modal shifts[67] in two areas are noteworthy: design perspective and approach (shifting between designer and user perspectives) and design activities or tools (changing between ways of engagement). As a result, the personal worldview, or frame of reference, of students is challenged.[68] The problem of sustaining a connected approach is also noteworthy, as the two-thirds of responses that are connected decline into a quarter of the class on the trajectory to completing the studio design project beyond the workshop.

Ways of engagement

The triangulated relationship of 'think', 'make' and 'share'[69] provides three categories of operational thought and critical reflection that students are accustomed to. They are able to shift amongst these spontaneously to expand their understanding and explore a human-centred perspective. 'Think' provides new insights when keywords and vignettes are used because of its immersive and situational focus. 'Make' reveals relational and symbolic associations through the vignette drawings and the making of critical arte-facts. The critical reflection allows students to 'share' with peers in order to unpack what human-centred design means to them and to reflect on its contextual meaning[70] and their understanding of it. In addition, it provides insight into how the community and its members are viewed and under-stood within the context of the city and in relation to one another. Human-centred values become visible through the students' initial understanding – a (momentary) shift in attitude to inclusivity, and the awareness of flexibility when spatial agency[71] is embedded in the design approach.

The two modes proving most difficult to engage are 'feel' and 'do'.[72] They relate to empathy, one value that proves challenging to activate and sustain.[73] The transition between 'connected' and 'separate' views[74] requires a different mindset that enables shifting from one to the other. In addition, the challenge concerning empathy is to balance affective and cognitive empathy and to complete the empathy phase by detaching[75] from matters often understood and internalised in a personal way. The data show that the minority of students sustains the modal shift to 'feel' and 'do', which both relate to transformative learning by taking conscious action and reevaluat-ing old ways.

Transformative learning

The shift from 'separate' to 'connected' ways of knowing[76] relates to the tra-jectory of transformation in students as individuals. The data analysis shows that Perry's developmental cycle provides a useful benchmark amongst 'mul-tiplicity', 'contextual relativism' and 'commitment'[77] for students in third-year design. Some find the unfamiliar approach too overwhelming and, while it takes time for them to adjust to a different mindset and new activities in the design studio, they may revert to 'multiplicity'.[78] However, the new approach also provides a springboard for extending into new realms of understanding, where a shift to 'commitment'[79] is visible. A quarter of the students choose, of their own accord, to include the workshop activities in the exam presen-tation at the end of the year, as one integrated design project. This actively displays their acceptance and conviction of human-centred values. Of the two students' journeys presented here, it is worth noting that only Student One integrated the workshop values by refocusing the attention on tempo-rality and diversity. The student adapted her point of view[80] by consider-ing the user's deep-seated needs, such as personal belonging and contextual interaction. For Student Two, this conscious line of thought ended with the workshop, with some intuitive slants towards meaning making through asso-ciations with materials in the studio design project. However, the richness and complexity expressed in the workshop and considerations of personal interactions and relational encounters were not assimilated, which raises the question of 'how' small shifts can be sustained beyond the workshop.

Concluding remarks

As an exploratory case study, the findings and observations presented here are preliminary. Completing the remaining three case studies as part of a larger future research project will provide a full scope of analysis and conclusions. However, as an initial investigation, this study reveals noteworthy observations related to the challenges and opportunities present, with evidence of modal shifts and an awareness of embedded complexity when the user's tangible and intangible needs are considered.

The study opens the dialogue on the importance of other ways of engagement in creative and critical inquiry in an architecture studio, emphasising the potential value of a situational prioritised human-centred approach.[81] It argues for a reevaluation of attitudes and values that prioritise the dynamic social aspects of human interaction and the relationships between people above physical building considerations in design. In this way, students are empowered as future practitioners with another skill set as praxis with a different focus, one that requires architects and designers to understand in other ways – not as experts only – but to formulate a deeper understanding of complex conditions and situations from the perspective of the user. As citizen designers,[82] students then become agents for spatial complexity and agency and for the fluid and unpredictable scenarios inscribed in design projects. It depends on the individual whether human-centred design values are assimilated as part of design engagement.

The speculative nature of the exploration raises some new questions. In the context of an inductive approach to the investigation, topics emerge that were not considered at the outset. Discursive design[83] and normative dissociation[84] are two examples. Discursive design can be considered as a newly formulated concept for creative practices, aiming to unlock discourse by asking critical questions through discursive objects, without solving any problems, but to provoke the audience to reflect on a message.[85] The critical artefacts fall within this approach, only discovered towards the end of the analysis phase. Early observations show that this approach, in conjunction with normative dissociation, where the designer assumes the role of the user through "absorption and imaginative involvement",[86] could shed a different light on transformative learning, especially where the "ideas and belief systems" of students are challenged.[87]

The main unknown – how to sustain small shifts towards a human-centred approach – remains, especially in the context of the case study where additional underlying requirements are embedded in three unidentified design project briefs, introducing other contexts, typologies, programmes and users to the remaining workshops. It is natural to revert to old habits and tried and tested methods. This speculative inquiry argues that traditional ways can no longer adequately address the complex challenges hidden in design projects.[88] Other ways of engagement, critical and creative, seem to unlock a more engaged way of learning. Once the focus shifts to the micro, it emphasises what lies under the surface, which is closer, finer and more subtle. It explores with an interior lens and requires more connection, albeit in the realm of the urban.

Notes

1 Robert K. Yin, *Case Study Research: Design and Methods* (Los Angeles: SAGE Publications, Inc.), 238.
2 Roger C. Fisher and Nicolas J. Clarke, "RED in Architecture: An Ecotropic Approach," *Innovate* 7 (2012): 72, accessed February 19, 2019, http://citeseerx.ist.psu.edu/viewdoc/download?doi=10.1.1.360.5231&rep=rep1&type=pdf.
3 Ashraf M. Salama, *Spatial Design Education: New Directions for Pedagogy in Architecture and Beyond* (Surrey: Ashgate Publishing Limited, 2015).
4 Salama, *Spatial Design Education*, 6.
5 Ibid.
6 Bruce Archer, "Design as a Discipline," *Design Studies* 1, no. 1 (1979): 17–20, accessed April 28, 2020, www.scribd.com.document/377567035/Archer-Bruce-Design-as-a-Discipline.
7 Salama, *Spatial Design Education*, 6.
8 Nishat Awan, Tatjana Schneider and Jeremy Till, *Spatial Agency: Other Ways of Doing Architecture* (London: Routledge, 2001), 32.
9 Jeremy Till, *Architecture Depends* (Cambridge, MA: The MIT Press, 2009), 104.
10 Awan et al., *Spatial Agency*, 31.
11 Till, *Architecture Depends*, 151.
12 Ibid.
13 Ibid., 178.
14 Ibid., 178–9.
15 Elizabeth Resnick, *Developing Citizen Designers* (New York: Bloomsbury Academic, 2016), 288.
16 Bryan Lawson, *How Designers Think: The Design Process Demystified* (London: Butterworth Architecture, 1990), 26.
17 Nigel Cross, "Designerly Ways of Knowing," *Design Studies* 3, no. 4 (1982): 226, accessed October 17, 2019, doi:10.1016/0142-694X(82)90040-0.
18 Till, *Architecture Depends*, 111.
19 Bella Martin and Bruce Hanington, *Universal Methods of Design: 125 Ways to Research Complex Problems, Develop Innovative Ideas, and Design Effective Solutions* (Beverly, MA: Rockport Publishers, 2019).
20 Till, *Architecture Depends*, 113.
21 Ibid.
22 Awan et al., *Spatial Agency*, 28.
23 Tim Brown, *Change by Design: How Design Thinking Transforms Organisations and Inspires Innovation* (New York: Harper Business, 2009), 50.

24 Don Norman, *The Design of Everyday Things* (New York: Basic Books, 1988/2013).
25 Brown, *Change by Design.*
26 "IDEO Human-Centered Design Toolkit," IDEO, accessed June, 9, 2019, www. designkit.org.
27 "The Design Process: What is the Double Diamond?" UK Design Council, accessed June 9, 2019, www.designcouncil.org.uk/news-opinion/design-process-what-double-diamond.
28 Ibid.
29 Maria Camacho, "An Integrative Model of Design Thinking" (paper presented at the 21st DMI: Academic Design Management Conference Next Wave, London, UK, August 1–2, 2018), accessed October 19, 2019, www.researchgate.net/publication/326990650_An_Integrative_Model_of_Design_Thinking.
30 Chris Luebkeman, "Design Is Our Answer: An Interview with Leading Design Thinker Tim Brown," *Architectural Design* 85, no. 4 (2015): 37, accessed October 29, 2019, doi:10.1002/ad1922.
31 Resnick, *Developing Citizen Designers*, 287.
32 Ibid.
33 Linda N. Laursen and Louise M. Haase, "The Shortcomings of Design Thinking When Compared to Designerly Thinking," *The Design Journal* 22, no. 6 (2019): 826, accessed October 15, 2019, doi:10.1080/14606925.2019.1652531.
34 Ibid., 827.
35 Resnick, *Developing Citizen Designers*, 288.
36 Brown, *Change by Design*, 50.
37 Paul Bloom, *Against Empathy: The Case for Rational Compassion* (London: The Bodley Head, 2016), 3, 9.
38 Merlijn Kouprie and Froukje Sleeswijk Visser, "A Framework for Empathy in Design: Stepping Into and Out of the User's Life," *Journal of Engineering Design* 20, no. 5 (2009): 442, accessed January 24, 2020, doi:10.1080./09544820902875033.
39 Hennie Reynders, "Gestural Topographies: A Framework for the Practice of Reflective and Critical Disruption" (paper presented at Swiss Design Network International Conference SDN, Disruptive Interaction, Lugano, November 9, 2012), 49–62, accessed October 23, 2018, www.academia.edu/2964329/Gestural_Topographies__a_framework_for_the_practice_of_reflective_and_critical_disruption, 13.
40 Fisher and Clarke, "RED in Architecture", 72–5.
41 Sashi Caan, *Rethinking Design and Interiors: Human Beings in the Built Environment* (London: Lawrence King Publishing, 2011), 53.
42 Clayton M. Christensen, *The Innovator's Dilemma: When New Technologies Cause Great Firms to Fail* (Boston, MA: Harvard Business Review Press, 1997/2016).
43 Layla Acaroglu, *Disruptive Design: A Method for Activating Positive Social Change by Design* (New York: Disrupt Design LLC, 2017).
44 Mary F. Belenky, Blythe M. Clinchy, Nancy R. Goldberger and Jull M. Tarule, *Women's Way of Knowing: The Development of Self, Voice and Mind* (New York: Basic Books, 1986/1997), 103, 112.
45 William G. Perry, *Forms of Ethical and Intellectual Development in the College Years: A Scheme* (San Francisco: Josey-Bass Inc., Publishers, 1970/1999), 57.
46 Nancy J. Evans et al., *Student Development in College: Theory, Research and Practice* (San Francisco: Jossey-Bass, 2010), 86–7.
47 Belenky et al., *Women's Way of Knowing.*
48 Evans et al., *Student Development in College*, 122.

49 Jack Mezirow, "Transformative Learning: Theory to Practice," *New Directions for Adult and Continuing Education* 74 (1997): 5–6, accessed November 11, 2019, doi:10.1002/ace.7401.
50 Perry, *Forms of Ethical*, 115.
51 Belenky et al., W*omen's Way*, 112.
52 Louis Cohen, Lawrence Manion and Keith Morrison, *Research Methods in Education* (London: Routledge, 2018), 23.
53 Robert Yin, *Qualitative Research from Start to Finish* (London: The Guilford Press, 2016), 160.
54 Ibid., 99–100.
55 John W. Creswell and Cheryl N. Poth, *Qualitative Inquiry and Research Design: Choosing Among Five Approaches* (Los Angeles: SAGE, 2018), 322.
56 Archer, "Design as a Discipline," 17–20.
57 Donald A. Schön, *The Reflective Practitioner: How Professionals Think in Action* (New York: Basic Books, 1983), 131–2.
58 Agaroglu, *Disruptive Design*.
59 Christensen, *An Innovator's Dilemma*.
60 Schön, *The Reflective Practitioner*, 59.
61 Yin, *Qualitative Research*, 199–200.
62 Russel H. Bernard and Gery W. Ryan, *Analyzing Qualitative Data: Systematic Approaches* (Los Angeles: SAGE, 2010), 192.
63 Resnick, *Developing Citizen Designers*, 288.
64 Belenky et al., *Women's Way*, 112.
65 Ibid., 103.
66 Till, *Architecture Depends*, 178.
67 Nigel Cross, *Designerly Ways of Knowing* (London: Springer-Verlag, 2006), 88.
68 Mezirow, "Transformative Learning," 5.
69 Reynders, "Gestural Topography," 13.
70 Klaus Krippendorff and Reinhart Butter, "Semantics: Meanings and Contexts of Artifacts," in *Product Experience*, ed. H. N. J. Schifferstein and P. Hekkert (New York, NY: Elsevier, 2007), 10–11, accessed April 28, 2020, http://repository.upenn.edu/asc_papers/91.
71 Awan et al., *Spatial Agency*, 31.
72 Fisher and Clarke, "RED in Architecture," 72–5.
73 Kouprie and Visser, "A Framework for Empathy," 439.
74 Belenky et al., *Women's Way*, 123–4.
75 Kouprie and Visser, "A Framework for Empathy," 446.
76 Belenky et al., *Women's Way*, 123–4.
77 Perry, *Forms of Ethical*, 57–8.
78 Ibid., 95, 109.
79 Ibid., 134.
80 Mezirow, "Transformative Learning," 6.
81 Resnick, *Developing Citizen Designers*, 288.
82 Ibid.
83 Bruce M. Tharp and Stephanie M. Tharp, *Discursive Design: Critical, Speculative and Alternative Things* (Cambridge, MA: The MIT Press, 2018).
84 Maria E. Panero, Landon Michaels and Ellen Winner, "Becoming a Character: Dissociation in Conservatory Acting Students," *Journal of Trauma and Dissociation* 21, no. 1 (2019), accessed November 11, 2019, doi:10.1080/15299732.2019.1675220.

85 Tharp and Tharp, *Discursive Design*, 112.
86 Panero et al., "Becoming a Character," 13.
87 Mezirow, "Transformative Learning," 11.
88 Salama, *Spatial Design Education*, 6.

Bibliography

Acaroglu, Leyla. *Disruptive Design: A Method for Activating Positive Social Change by Design.* New York: Disrupt Design LLC, 2017.

Archer, Bruce. "Design as a Discipline." *Design Studies* 1, no. 1 (1979): 17–20. Accessed April 28, 2020. www.scribd.com/document/377567035/Archer-Bruce-Design-as-a-Discipline.

Awan, Nishat, Tatjana Schneider, and Jeremy Till. *Spatial Agency: Other Ways of Doing Architecture.* London: Routledge, 2001.

Belenky, Mary F., Blythe M. Clinchy, Nancy R. Goldberger, and Jill M. Tarule. *Women's Way of Knowing: The Development of Self, Voice and Mind.* New York: Basic Books, 1986.

Bernard, H. Russel, and Gery W. Ryan. *Analyzing Qualitative Data: Systematic Approaches.* Los Angeles: SAGE Publications, 2010.

Bloom, Paul. *Against Empathy: The Case for Rational Compassion.* London: The Bodley Head, 2016.

Brown, Tim. *Change by Design: How Design Thinking Transforms Organisations and Inspires Innovation.* New York: Harper Business, 2009.

Caan, Sashi. *Rethinking Design and Interiors: Human Beings in the Built Environment.* London: Lawrence King Publishing, 2011.

Camacho, Maria. "An Integrative Model of Design Thinking." Paper presented at the *21st DMI: Academic Design Management Conference Next Wave*, London, UK, August 1–2, 2018, 627–41. Accessed October 19, 2019. www.researchgate.net/publication/326990650_An_Integrative_Model_of_Design_Thinking.

Christensen, Clayton M. *An Innovator's Dilemma.* Cambridge, MA: Harvard Business Review, 1997.

Cohen, Louis, Lawrence Manion, and Keith Morrison. *Research Methods in Education.* London: Routledge, 2018.

Cooley, M. *Architect or Bee?* Boston: South End Press, 1982.

Creswell, John W., and Cheryl N. Poth. *Qualitative Inquiry and Research Design: Choosing among Five Approaches.* Los Angeles: SAGE Publications, 2018.

Cross, Nigel. "Designerly Ways of Knowing." *Design Studies* 3, no. 4 (1982): 221–7. Accessed October 17, 2019. doi:10.1016/0142-694X(82)90040-0.

Cross, Nigel. *Designerly Ways of Knowing.* London: Springer-Verlag, 2006.

Evans, Nancy, J., Deanna S. Forney, Florence M. Guido, Lori D. Patton, and Kristen A. Renn. *Student Development in College: Theory, Research and Practice.* San Francisco: Jossey-Bass, 2010.

Fisher, Roger C., and Nicolas J. Clarke. "RED in Architecture: An Ecotropic Approach." *Innovate* 7 (2012): 72–5. Accessed February 19, 2019. http://citeseerx.ist.psu.edu/viewdoc/download?doi=10.1.1.360.5231&rep=rep1&type=pdf.

IDEO. "IDEO Human-Centered Design Toolkit." Accessed June, 9, 2019. www. designkit.org.

Kouprie, Merlijn, and Froukje S. Visser. "A Framework for Empathy in Design: Stepping Into and Out of the User's Life." *Journal of Engineering Design* 20, no. 5 (2009): 437–48. Accessed January 24, 2020. doi:10.1080./09544820902875033.

Krippendorff, Klaus, and Reinhart Butter. "Semantics: Meanings and Contexts of Artifacts." In *Product Experience*, edited by H.N.J. Schifferstein and P. Hekkert, 1–27. New York, NY: Elsevier, 2007. Accessed April 28, 2020. http://repository. upenn.edu/asc_papers/91.

Laursen, Linda N., and Louise M. Haase. "The Shortcomings of Design Thinking When Compared to Designerly Thinking." *The Design Journal* 22, no. 6 (2019): 813–32. Accessed October 15, 2019. doi:10.1080/14606925.2019.1652531.

Lawson, Bryan. *How Designers Think: The Design Process Demystified*. London: Butterworth Architecture, 1990.

Luebkeman, Chris. "Design Is Our Answer: An Interview with Leading Design Thinker Tim Brown." *Architectural Design* 85, no. 4 (2015): 34–9. Accessed October 29, 2019. doi:10.1002/ad1922.

Martin, Bella, and Bruce Hanington. *Universal Methods of Design: 125 Ways to Research Complex Problems, Develop Innovative Ideas, and Design Effective Solutions*. Beverly, MA: Rockport Publishers, 2019.

Mezirow, Jack. "Transformative Learning: Theory to Practice." *New Directions for Adult and Continuing Education* 74 (1997): 5–12. Accessed November 11, 2019. doi:10.1002/ace.7401.

Norman, Don. *The Design of Everyday Things*. New York: Basic Books, 1988/2013.

Panero, Maria E., Landon Michaels, and Ellen Winner. "Becoming a Character: Dissociation in Conservatory Acting Students." *Journal of Trauma and Dissociation* 21, no. 1 (2019): 87–102. Accessed November 11, 2019. doi:10.1080/15299732 .2019.1675220.

Perry, William G. *Forms of Ethical and Intellectual Development in the College Years: A Scheme*. San Francisco: Josey-Bass Inc. Publishers, 1970.

Resnick, Elizabeth. *Developing Citizen Designers*. New York: Bloomsbury Academic, 2016.

Reynders, Hennie. "Gestural Topographies: A Framework for the Practice of Reflective and Critical Disruption." Paper presented at *Swiss Design Network International Conference SDN*, Disruptive Interaction, Lugano, November 9, 2012, 49–62. Accessed October 23, 2018. www.academia.edu/2964329/Gestural_ Topographies_-_a_framework_for_the_practice_of_reflective_and_critical_ disruption.

Salama, Ashraf M. *Spatial Design Education: New Directions for Pedagogy in Architecture and Beyond*. Surrey: Ashgate Publishing Limited, 2015.

Schön, Donald A. *The Reflective Practitioner: How Professionals Think in Action*. New York: Basic Books, 1983.

Tharp, Bruce M., and Stephanie M. Tharp. *Discursive Design: Critical Speculative and Alternative Things*. Cambridge, MA: The MIT Press, 2018.

Till, Jeremy. *Architecture Depends*. Cambridge, MA: The MIT Press, 2009.

UK Design Council. "The Design Process: What Is the Double Diamond?" Accessed June 9, 2019. www.designcouncil.org.uk/news-opinion/design-process-what-double-diamond.

Yin, Robert K. *Case Study Research: Design and Methods*. Los Angeles: SAGE Publications, 2014.

Yin, Robert K. *Qualitative Research from Start to Finish*. New York: The Guilford Press, 2016.

4 Collaborative thinking through the dynamics of site and architecture in design education

Sean Burns

Introduction

Designing for a complex world requires architects to think critically, creatively, and collaboratively. To support the development of this skill set, the atmosphere of the design studio in architectural education challenges students to creatively develop ideas and critically reflect upon their conceptual designs for given projects. In design education, thinking collaboratively does not need to be solely defined by the sharing of ideas and information among peers, but instead can be applied to how architecture and its site might collectively inform one another throughout the design process to achieve a desired solution.

Often, students are taught to sequentially operate within the design process by observing, recording, and then responding to its site conditions towards formulating an architectural intervention. This procedure, while beneficial in teaching students to acknowledge and appreciate the contextual environment as an essential component of their design, can be misguided as it emphasises the site as a given, invariable constraint that is static and impermeable in nature. Architectural design involves a mediation of the designer's intentions with the site. As such, students should be encouraged to consider architecture and all atmospheric conditions of the site – within, among, and beyond the confines of an accepted ground plane – as malleable and accommodating bodies.

This chapter present a series of speculative projects, introduced to students in their second year of study within an accredited undergraduate architectural curriculum, that advocate for a departure from any prescribed design methodology and, instead, investigate opportunities to promote a responsive dialogue between architecture and site throughout the design process. At the outset of each project, students were asked to blur the demarcations of architecture and site, among the earth and beyond to the sky, towards discovering ways in which architecture and its contextual surroundings might respect, respond, and support one another to cultivate a desired user experience. These exercises offered students an avenue to creatively and critically manoeuver the design process while promoting collaborative thinking between architecture and its environment.

Questioning how we perceive the environment

Architectural design is a nonlinear process in which students are frequently asked to continually reconsider their design decisions in an effort to iterate and variate conceptual parameters prior to arriving at a final solution. At the outset of a project, where initial site analysis is paramount, the value of this negotiation is at risk of being abandoned as students often gather pertinent information concerning the discovered characteristics of a site, which are then inventoried as a catalogue of existing site properties, prior to engaging in the design of an architectural intervention. This process entails the acceptance of a site's existing conditions as a permanent constraint, resolute in its capabilities to be altered or moulded to best accommodate the desires of an architectural proposition.

Throughout the environment, relationships among systems and elements are unresolved and complex in nature. To perceive and recognise these interactions effectively requires designers to establish a value system predicated upon an awareness and informed response to the contextual environment. Art historian and theorist Gyorgy Kepes designates our body as "the basic instrument that we use to make our experience intelligible. With it, we articulate the constant stream of impressions on our senses, differentiating the world into discrete entities and unifying it into an interrelated whole."[1] Here, Kepes introduces "axes of reference," asserted as a set of values for how we authentically observe, organise, and understand the world intelligently.[2] This common denominator directly influences our modes of discovery and awareness of the environment, which Kepes categorises as a three-stage process that we undergo throughout life, centred upon our perceived comparisons of objects and their respective contextual settings. In our youth, we substantiate all identities in the world through 'dynamic relation seeing' where we see things through their potential for practical use. As we mature, we relinquish these associations based on our familiarities of entities and enter the phase 'thing seeing,' where we focus primarily on the static characteristics of objects, notably the size, shape, colour, and substance, of encountered articles. In order to appreciate a world of complex configurations, Kepes urges us to revisit our youthful mode of perceiving the environment to acknowledge "interactions rather than things" and ultimately realise a sense of 'pattern seeing,' whereby we might "trace the interplay of processes in the world" rather than "refer everything to our narrow subjective life."[3]

Anthropologist Tim Ingold argues that to study the development and evolution of life effectively commands that we not focus solely on the physiological characteristics of society and cultures. Instead, Ingold formulates a theoretical approach to anthropology based on studying relationships and appreciating life's processes of growth and movement.[4] Here, Ingold suggests we view the world as an entanglement of persuasive and interacting lines by asserting "people inhabit a world that consists, in the first place, not of things but of lines . . . to study both people and things is to study the lines they are made of."[5]

The messages of both Kepes and Ingold specifically urge us to sense the world *intelligently* by advocating we abandon any predetermined, or engrained, associations between object and its contextual field as conditions that are static, permanent, and/or independent of one another. Instead, we should entertain the world as an evolutionary arena where nature's entries and all interceding artifacts are in continual communication to forge essential bonds and establish collaborative relationships within the contextual environment. Here, designers are encouraged to reconsider their systematic approach for how they perceive their surroundings to allow for a prolonged dialogue among architecture and its situational context throughout the iterative design process. Gevork Hartoonian stresses that "Architecture is relentlessly reformulating itself according to formal and contextual factors."[6] Hartoonian's writings imply that a given site's context is fluid, tolerate, and assertive in its ability to inform architectural manoeuvers throughout the continuum of architectural design. As such, designers should discount any preconceived notions of architecture as a subservient instrument to its contextual environment and reevaluate the hierarchical relationship between site and architecture. Ultimately, Hartoonian's message necessitates designers to embrace all atmospheric qualities of a given site, above and below the earth's surface, as collaborative and persuasive agents throughout the design process. No longer should object reside over its surrounding field, nor should a site's contextual forces strictly dictate any operations for architectural design.

Examining the earth's terrain as sensible and active substance

The term *terrain* is generally categorised as a set of residual field conditions along the earth's surface, produced by the interactions of geological land formations within a general region. This definition unfairly emphasises terrain as an undulating ground plane, examined at a broad scale, derived by the locale's historical development. Thus, the acceptance of these defining characteristics limit the ability of terrain to assume the role as a facilitator for design at a localised site within an architectural project. Architectural theorist David Leatherbarrow has written extensively on the perceptions and implications of terrain as an intermediary of landscape and architectural design as he states that terrain "has the power to allow and to resist the dislocations we experience today, recalling what a location has been while indicating what it is becoming."[7] Reassessing the definition and representational qualities of terrain necessitates that we explore its potential involvement within the design process for any proposed architectural act relative to all atmospheric conditions of a site – above and beneath the ground plane. To accomplish this, designers must reconsider terrain as an expression of the earth's substantial disposition at a scale more closely aligned with a project's site in order to allow it to become an integral article of design, equally concerned with the continuity and further progression of the earth's composition as much as its prior historical maturation.

The writings of architectural theorist Lars Spuybroek offer insight to allow us to successfully reexamine terrain as an impressionable substance, rather than as a reactive surface. In his disdain for how we critically accept and evaluate contemporary architecture, Spuybroek urges designers to explore a materialistic interpretation and appreciation of aesthetics as a means to effectively understand and interpret our experiences of "an architecture generated from active matter."[8] The body is of primary concern for Spuybroek's aesthetic theory as it is the essential medium to provide coherence for our surroundings; "experience counts as the main form of involvement, and when looking at architecture, tectonics counts as the main form of articulation."[9] Spuybroek references the works of philosopher Denis Diderot, who deemed all genuine beings discovered in life, whether natural or artificial, as *sensitive* and *irritable matter* to support his model of an 'aesthetic experience,' by which "the sensed, the seen, and the structured share the same continuum."[10] Applying the philosophical messages of Spuybroek and Diderot to architectural design suggest that the earth's terrain might be reinterpreted as an active matter, empathetic, sensible, and accommodating of any proposed or constructed architectural edifice to provide an authentic and site-specific designed experience.

Defining territory: the earth's role as a negotiated surface or malleable substance

Territory implies an entity's ownership with strict and implicit boundaries among contiguous domains. As such, the imposition and authorship of all territorial metes and boundary conditions must be negotiated in a codependent, rational, and thoughtful manner to allow for an architectural intervention to become a memorable place, as opposed to a nondescript space that occupies its setting. A terrain's topography provides unbiased and pragmatic demarcations among regions towards establishing and fortifying affected social, governmental, economic, and/or political territories. According to Bernard Cache, the formalistic constraints that emanate from various folds within the earth's terrain directly influence the organisational, identifiable, and accessible possibilities of architecture among articulated territories, yet these features of the earth are dynamic, with respect to our physical acknowledgement and metaphysical comprehension of the engaged environment: "the surface of a territory is mobile and fluid as it is given to the distortions of memory."[11] Similarly, Leatherbarrow provides insight for how implied and realised patterns of movement, interpreted boundary conditions, and the calibration of topographical formations are common parameters for landscape and architectural design. "*Flow*, the central concept of contemporary (architectural) spatiality, takes extended *territory* (landscape) as its basic premise."[12] Leatherbarrow challenges the passages within *Erste Natur* by Edmund Husserl to reveal methods for how the territorial boundaries of the earth are no longer limited, or defined, solely by its topographical surface, but instead must acknowledge the concept of the earth as 'an unelaborated substrate.' Too often, "topography persists as a remnant in finished works, a remainder that resists complete cultivation, finishing or articulation, a neglected capacity that 'might break through' just because it is *regellos*."[13] Instead,

> Figuration uses, but does not sever the ties between the object and this substrate, for topography has the power to continually reform what has been formed, unsettling previously settled arrangements. Construction finishing in both landscape and architecture takes advantage of this potential in its care for the inner capacities of things.[14]

Ilka and Andreas Ruby underscore the rediscovery of the ground as a vital intermediary for architectural design, where figure–ground and solid–void relationships must be interrogated towards establishing a harmonic coexistence, and effective relationship, among architecture and its situated context. Twentieth-century modernism consistently neutralised the ground plane, accepting an attitude to champion architecture as an isolated and heroic object, unconcerned with its contextual surroundings or any historical associations to influence design.[15] Vittorio Gregotti stated that "The worst enemy of modern architecture is the idea of space, considered solely in terms of economic and technical exigencies indifferent to the ideas of the site."[16] For Gregotti, the earth's surface and substance assumes a responsibility to inform any architectural intervention, "before placing stone on stone, man placed the stone on the ground to recognise a site in the midst of an unknown universe, in order to take account of it and modify it."[17] Ilka and Andreas Ruby validate Gregotti's assertion through their presentation of various categorical studies for how the earth might be fundamentally regarded and actively engaged as a soft body, or pliable surface, in association with contemporary architectural design.

> In order to treat the ground as more than just an earth-encompassing skin of the territory where spatial objects are positioned, we must treat the ground itself as a spatial body – i.e. distinguish the ground from the sheer endless surface of the territory and frame it as a finite entity.[18]

Further, their writings support the blurring of any distinctions among the built environment and its abiding natural contextual surroundings as an opportunity to allow for the earth's terrain, and subsequently assumed territories, to be liberated from the domination of architecture as an independent object residing over its field. Instead, "the void between building and ground condenses to become a real space that defines the relationship between architecture and territory."[19] Collectively, these messages advocate for a site's conditions to primarily operate receptively and collaboratively among all adjoining architectural obligations throughout all phases of the architectural design process. Thus, architecture assumes the role of a compromising agent, incessantly compelled to unify the built and natural conditions of the contextual environment towards creating a site-specific experience for its designated user.

Negotiation of the earth through tectonic and stereotomic processes

Strategies for engaging and collaborating with the ground require architects to contemplate the compositional materialisation of the earth in equal valuation to the design, configuration, positioning, and desirable orientation of an intended architectural gesture. In architectural design, the earth is often unduly perceived as a strict demarcated topographical line that is void of thickness and solely representative of nature's boundary conditions. Leatherbarrow states that "topography is the topic architecture and landscape architecture hold in common."[20] Further, "topography is neither land nor form," as it "gives itself to experience in a paradoxical way, (that which is) manifestly latent. . . . It does not intentionally expose the grounds of its formation, but serves as the grounds for that formation."[21] Here, Leatherbarrow argues for agency to exist within the marriage of site and architecture: as collaborating entities that are either passive or assertive in nature.

"When a landscape or building shows itself, topography is not annulled, only sublimated, for it continues to exist at the margins of, or beneath, all that invites attention."[22] Ultimately Leatherbarrow argues that "topography must not be limited to a record of the existing profile of a site but must also incorporate terrain, both built and unbuilt."[23] Thus, topography becomes the arbitrator of the site to enable designers to explore the territorial composition among landscape and architecture. Tomà Berlanda supports this argument by stressing that the arrangement amidst the earth and any mediating artifact should be considered as a solidarity agreement between built and natural development, rather than isolative in nature.[24]

Eradicating the muted voice of a site mandates designers to recognise the earth as an active participant within the architectural design process. The acceptance of this conceptual framework liberates designers from perceiving the earth and accompanying architecture as disparate entities, thus, encouraging architects to contemplate how the imposition of a built structure might be successfully deployed to symbiotically occupy its contextual surroundings beneath, among, and beyond the earth's formations. The terms tectonics and stereotomics offer credence to methodological approaches for engaging the earth as a negotiable plane or impressionable soft substance within architectural design.

In his writing about the works of Karl Bötticher, Stanford Anderson states that tectonics "refer not just to the activity of making the materially requisite construction that answer certain needs, but rather to the activity that raises this construction to an art form."[25] Gottfried Semper defined tectonics as one of the four raw material classifications of architectural theory, identified by the inherent attributes, technical purpose, and artistic craft required to enable a framework to "embody the highest and most universal theme of architecture."[26] The assemblage of frame within Semper's classification acknowledges the art and science of architectural design and construction, with specific attention placed on the articulation of joint conditions among structural formwork elements as arranged through an additive processes. By comparison, Semper addresses the subject of stereotomy as construction procedures that are consequential to architectural design and aligned with the stacking of repetitious heavy units, sourced from the earth's material substance, to support the tectonic interferences of architecture.[27]

Kenneth Frampton contends that architectural tectonics correlate to the temporary lightweight frame associated with the sky, where stereotomic features in architectural design are defined by their association with the permanent and immovable features of a site's conditions.[28] The writings of Hartoonian proclaim that the implementation of tectonic processes within architectural design should not be reduced to either a formal expression of construction methods or a representation of serviceable structural necessities that provide validation to form. Instead, Hartoonian states that, "It can be inferred that between the structural utility of architectonic elements and their analogical representation, there is a 'void,' so to speak, where the tectonic resides. This void molds architectural knowledge, that is the logos of making."[29]

Robin Evans presents the argument that stereotomy is etymological derived as the science of cutting solids.[30] Thus, stereotomic processes involve subtractive methodological procedures applied to the earth, in comparison to the additive techniques of assembling earth-governing materials, akin to Semper and Frampton's descriptions. Francesco Cacciatore supports Evans' theory through his survey of Louis Kahn's architectural operations and manipulations of solid and physical poché to reveal all consequential thickness of surviving mass among its material: "the real starting point in the process of expression and representation of this architecture is not the purely geometric and constructive dimension of the wall but rather its matter."[31] In support of this position, Juan González and José Castellón state,

> [I]f the tectonic approach puts the emphasis on the constructive and technical aspects of the building and on the expression of the detail, the stereotomic approach is grounded on the generation of the voids and on the definition of the boundaries of the building. In this way, the accumulation and distribution of matter produces at the same time both space and structure.[32]

Constructing site as a collaborator of architectural design

Following is a survey of preliminary and theoretical exercises, presented to second-year undergraduate architectural students as independent opportunities to reconsider any predetermined notions of architecture. To begin each project, students were asked to reevaluate any methodological approaches for design, specifically pertaining to the practice of acknowledging, recording, and responding to their presented surroundings. Instead, the students were urged to demonstrate strategical opportunities to promote the collaboration between an anticipated architectural solution and its situational environment. To best accomplish this goal, students were compelled to explore their authentic interpreted messages of the aforementioned passages related to environmental perceptions, terrain, territorial domains, topographical formations, stereotomy, and tectonic processes as inspirational messages for developing intentional procedural operations to celebrate the unification of proposed architectural artifacts among a situated context. This approach challenged each student to formulate a distinctive value system for how they might approach the atmospheric conditions of a site and execute a thoughtful architectural intervention that is harmoniously aligned, and in constant dialogue, with its collaborative environment throughout the iterative design process.

Each of the described projects commanded students to design and construct an imaginative site, conceived and guided by strategic additive, subtractive, or displacement operations, to ultimately accept an accommodating architectural imposition in a sympathetic manner. To successfully address this prescribed unification between object and its circumstantial field, students were asked to reflect upon the writings of Lars Spuybroek, who states that sympathy is a formation communicated by the "feeling that operates in the interstices of things," uniquely achieved among the unification of elements as a conditional expression of "what things feel when they shape one another."[33]

"The Plinth and the Tower"

A project entitled "The Plinth and the Tower" commenced by requesting students to fabricate a permeable scape, comprising various wood molding trim pieces, each with distinctive cross-sectional profiles, and assembled in a manner that resulted in the undulation of implied surface conditions along the x-y-z axes. Through their design and construction of the permeable scape, the students were asked to introduce a minimum of one distinct swollen protrusion and one depressed segment along the uppermost physical surface of its compositional formation. Produced through an additive process in the arrangement of incompatible elements with dissimilar lengths, the emergent landscape became a three-dimensional substance with frequent transitions occurring between porous cavities among dense solid mass clusters throughout its realised composition. Upon fabrication of the created site, the students were asked to study the generated effects from shadows and highlights along their permeable scape and assign a directional ordinance system for this aggregated contextual environment to further investigate in the subsequent portion of the project. The intention of this first stage of the exercise was to provide the students an opportunity to design and fabricate a site as an evolutionary body to convey the message that the earth is a soft and penetrable substance extending beneath its cover.

Phase two of the project asked the students to provide a disturbance to their generated site to accommodate specified programmatic requirements based on their previous light studies, activate a unifying descriptive design language, and demonstrate strategies to blur the territorial bounds between site and an architectural interference. Within this phase, the students were directed to investigate and incorporate two distinctive elemental archetypes – a *plinth* and a *tower* – and explore any potential exhibited behaviours among these fundamental components in accordance with their previously designed permeable scape. Identified as a robust and heavy base, the plinth embodied the intervention between earth and sky as it provided support for any prospective architectural element beyond its ordained mass. Engaging and emanating from the plinth, students were asked to propose a design for a tower structure to dominate the atmosphere beyond the permeable scape. The tower component was to be representative of a delicate structure, systematically organised through horizontal and vertical tectonic elements, to extend volumetric spaces and circulation channels in a logical sequence (Figure 4.1). To promote these messages, the plinth was required to penetrate the voids of the porous scape and sympathetically adjoin and/or buttress itself to the underlying components of the amalgamated site at various depths determined to ensure its stability. As such, the students were asked to design and fabricate the plinth as an element tolerant of the tower and capable of being removed from the permeable scape, motivating the students to design secure connections without the assistance of adhesive materials.

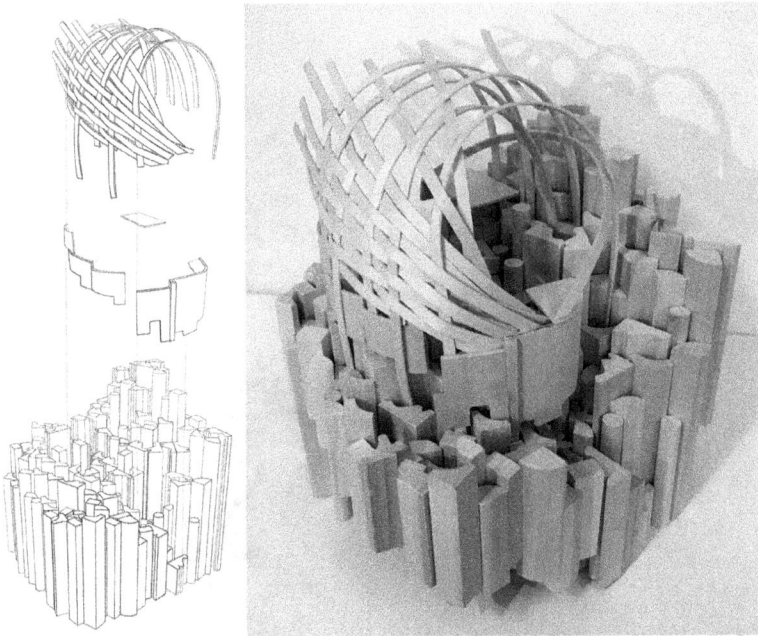

Figure 4.1 "Tower and the Plinth" final drawing study and physical model by student Eric Peters

"Instigating Slab"

Prior to beginning a project entitled "Instigating Slab," students were probed to analyse a selection of architectural precedents to determine potential relationships for how their interpretations of the provided readings related to tectonic and stereotomy processes might be acknowledged as strategies to implement a site-specific architectural creation. The students were explicitly asked to demonstrate evidence for how their comprehension of these terms might translate to approaches to architectural design that forge a poetic relationship between an architectural creation and its circumstantial landforms as part of the presentation materials for their chosen case study (Figure 4.2). Throughout this process, a vast majority of the students abandoned their impressed preconceptions of architectural design that focused on the external appearance of architecture and, instead, exhibited enthusiasm to further engage in conversations about the roles, relationships, and preparation of architecture amidst a cooperative site within the design process.

Equipped with the lessons of their precedent studies, students were asked to begin the design exercise by drawing a three-dimensional view of a nondescript mass parcel with specified dimensional attributes. Upon

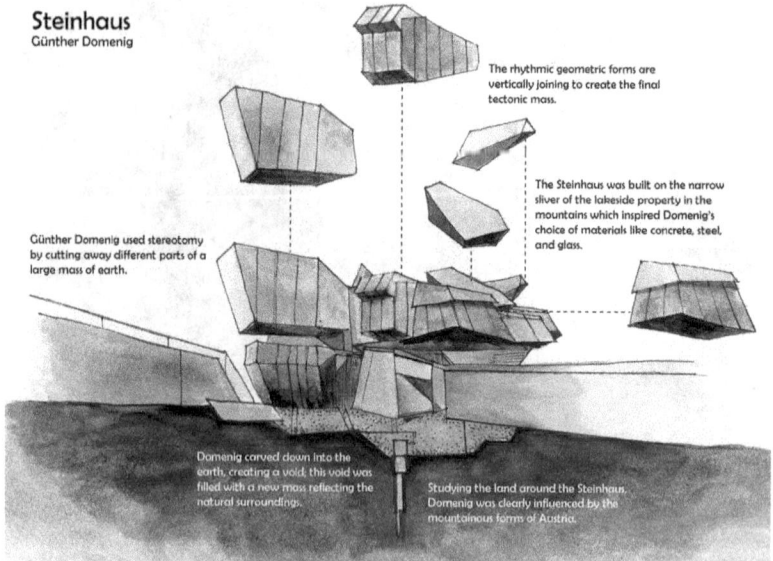

Steinhaus
Günther Domenig

The rhythmic geometric forms are vertically joining to create the final tectonic mass.

The Steinhaus was built on the narrow sliver of the lakeside property in the mountains which inspired Domenig's choice of materials like concrete, steel, and glass.

Günther Domenig used stereotomy by cutting away different parts of a large mass of earth.

Domenig carved down into the earth, creating a void, this void was filled with a new mass reflecting the natural surroundings.

Studying the land around the Steinhaus, Domenig was clearly influenced by the mountainous form of Austria.

Figure 4.2 Precedent study of Steinhaus by Günther Domenig by second-year students Samantha Felling and Nolan Furgye

establishing this initial drawing, the students were directed to subtract and reallocate portions of the slab's substance in a manner to suggest how a scaled figure might occupy areas of their proposal. The design for the final mass formation was prohibited from resting as a level object upon a pre-determined base, as all surface conditions of the parcel were required to show evidence of exhibited design operations. Following a review process of their drawings, the students were asked to cast their composite entity in plaster as a representation of a speculative site for further exploration as an active design agent in the subsequent phase of the project. Plaster was chosen as a medium for this stage of the project as it provided design students an opportunity to depart from traditional methods of assembling models through additive processes, commonly achieved by erecting or lay-ering rigid board pieces to represent architectural surfaces and contours that compose a site's topographical formation. Instead, the act of casting plaster provided an opportunity for students to envision the site as an evolutionary body, continually capable of being refined through additive (recasting) and subtractive processes (carving) throughout the design process.

The second phase of the project asked the students to reconsider the position and orientation of their excavated slab and incorporate multiple systematic tectonic framework assemblies among their design. The design of these inter-positions was to suggest, accentuate, and extend spaces, within and beyond the confines of the casted site, towards satisfying the programmatic require-ments for the design exercise. Students were asked to anticipate and deploy logical tectonic networks as a theatrical performance of ontological compo-nents to simultaneously ensure structural integrity and distinguish the bound-aries of the introduced volumetric spatial conditions among their envisioned design. For this phase, any presented tectonic system was to be compatible and responsive to the malleable site composition. To encourage the territorial boundary conditions of the earth and all imposed architectural activities to be perceived as indistinct constituents of the design process, the students were prohibited from using adhesive to adjoin the tectonic frames to encountered mass formations among the body of the site. Alternatively, the students were encouraged to consider sympathetic strategies to effectively connect frame-work assemblies to the earth's stereotomic substance (Figure 4.3).

"Tectonic Interventions"

A project entitled "Tectonic Interventions" incorporated many similar aspects of the project "Instigating Slab," as both design exercises com-menced by asking students to imagine a theoretical contextual site predi-cated through subtractive and displacement operations. Conceived as an abbreviated adaptation of "Instigating Slab," this project was intended to

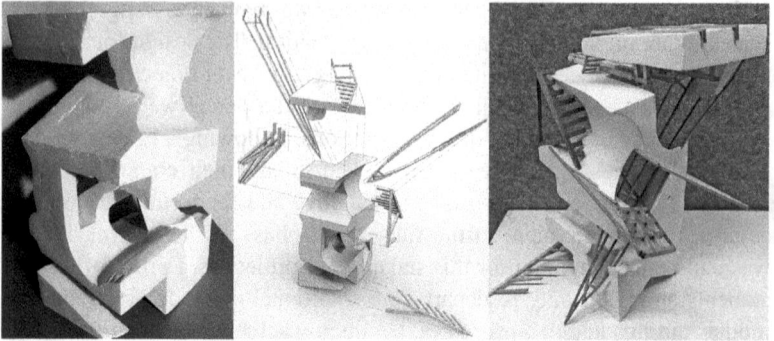

Figure 4.3 Progression of "Instigating Slab" project from casted slab, conceptual drawing for proposed tectonic intervention, final physical model representation by student Jake Nolan

accelerate the introduction of tectonic and stereotomy theories and entice students to reflect upon their values of architectural design. Specifically, the project provoked students to critically reconsider the perception of an environment's atmospheric surroundings as a sacred inventory of existing conditions for a project's site. Similar to the previous design exercise, the students were first exposed to relevant precedent studies as a means to better understand how tectonics and stereotomic procedures were understood and translated from theory to developed form within a compliant field.

Students began the project by creating a diagrammatic virtual model of a solid mass. While the mass was to be calibrated to explicit dimensional parameters that varied along each of its axes, the students were given the option to choose which measurement they wanted to apply to the height, width, and length of their initial design of the mass. Upon establishing, orientating, and positioning this solid abstract, the students were asked to envision this entity as a theoretical site and begin to introduce voids among its substance to host a scaled figure and promote circulation arteries throughout the stereotomic body. To guide the interferences of carved voids and displaced forms among their anticipated site, the students were required to consider incorporating a logical sequence of 'entry-passage-place' as a strategy to direct their operative design decisions for this preliminary stage of the project.

The second phase of the project compelled students to introduce rhythmic tectonic assemblies, within or beyond the margins of the articulated site, to direct passage and reconsider all boundary conditions for the prospective inhabitable volumetric spaces of their previously generated design. All installations of tectonic framework systems were intended to be complimentary and reactionary to the site in an effort to formulate a mutual relationship between a delivered object and its resounding field. This proposed resolution was deliberately aimed at enhancing the end user's experience by confirming an alliance between architectural elements and a collaborative site. Unlike the previous exercise, students were given the opportunity to determine when to manufacture their site and assemble the integral tectonic interventions within the duration of the project. Further, students were afforded autonomy in choosing fabrication procedures and representative materials to physically characterise the environment and any imposed framework devices for their project. These liberties often resulted in students revisiting their previous drawing studies as an instrument to attune the participatory inclusion of interceding additive elements among their conceptual design (Figure 4.4).

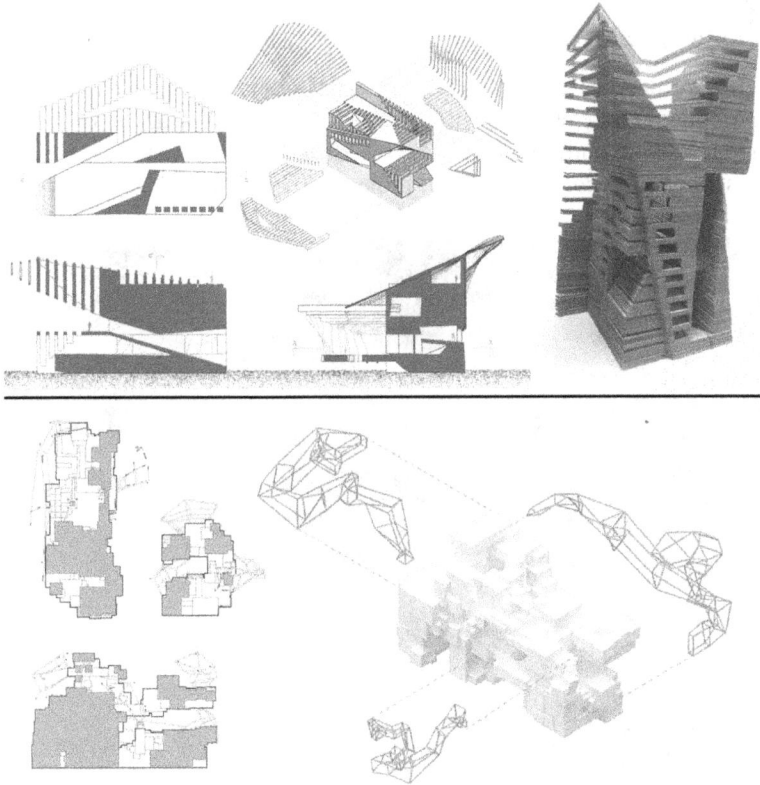

Figure 4.4 "Tectonic Intervention" drawings and studies by students Alex Tyson (top) and Maarten Bergsma (bottom)

To realise the project as a physical entity, a majority of the students opted to employ additive operations, as achieved through 3D printing processes or through stacking successive planar elements, to concurrently fabricate the assortment of tectonic configurations and their designed setting (Figure 4.5). While this method of constructing the site synchronously with all tectonic interventions as a mutual physical entity somewhat limited the capacity of expressing the field as an evolutionary body, it successfully interrogated the presence of territorial boundaries between the earth and any intervening architectural systems. Here, architecture and the compositional disposition of the earth were examined by their topological constituents to successfully achieve a solution for this design exercise. The lessons of this exercise encouraged students to further investigate the earth as a dynamic article of design and reassess the measure for how, and when, they might propose an architectural intervention among a given situational environment.

"Woven Terrain"

While the previous three exercises inspired students to reconsider their preconceptions of architecture and its position as a governing agent for design among its surroundings, it was observed that there exists an unintentional prescribed sequence in each of the projects for how the students first create

Figure 4.5 "Tectonic Intervention" final physical model by student Maarten Bergsma

an emergent site and then introduce an architectural response. As a reaction to these concerns, a project entitled "Woven Terrain" was conceived to reverse this design narrative while maintaining the message of site as a collaborative body, capable of influencing architecture throughout the design process. For this design exercise, the creation of formal tectonic components initially assumed the role as an instigating agent of design, capable of persuasively guiding representative operations to displace and/ or manipulate the mass formations of a site. Despite the project beginning with the establishment of an architectural creation prior to the interference of a responsive site, the students were motivated to continually regulate the control of each entity as a means to direct their design manoeuvers towards creating a dynamic situational environment throughout the project. The intention of this proposed approach was to strengthen the perception of a terrain's topographical nature as an empowered and integral participant throughout the architectural design process, instead of being expressed as a neglected and residual artifact of a completed architectural project.

The first phase of the project began by asking the students to prepare a drawing of a two-dimensional grid, one square foot in area with spaces between intersections no larger than three inches in any direction. Students were then prompted to raise and exploit the level grid as a three-dimensional form that demonstrated the behaviours of two descriptive action verbs of their choice. The performance of these informative terms was to be expressed as a physical manifestation of linear tectonic elements to establish an organisational frame, capable of being exploited, as a mediating constituent for the following portion of the design exercise. Upon fabricating the systematic skeleton as a material construct, the students were required to dedicate a north ordinance for their project, based on a specified locale, and explore how light might interface with their designed frame throughout the day.

For the second phase of the project, the students were charged to consider the produced effects of their previous light studies to conduct instances of space and passage for a scaled figure to occupy and transverse about a circumstantial environment. A variety of spatial conditions, ranging from embracing direct exposure of sunlight to providing protection within nested areas, were required to be exhibited among their final design solutions. To produce these specified functional volumetric spaces and suggestive modes of passage along the x-y-z axes of their formwork, the students were asked to weave a stereotomic terrain amongst the framed elements of their adopted design and explore all solid/void configurations throughout this evolving contextual substance. As the students began the design and induction of a representational terrain, they were encouraged to escape the confines of the tectonic framework to satisfy the functional requirements of the project. Further, the terrain's topographical formation was to respond to the actions of the frame, yet the students were permitted to adjust and recalibrate the arbitrating components of the tectonic assembly, as needed, to arrive at an optimal design solution.

Student proposals for the intertwining ground-scape demonstrated a variety of connection strategies for how the proposed earth's substance might rely upon, or absorb, the tectonic framework elements to support their design proposal. These implemented detail tactics pressed the students to consider the qualities of thickness, as related to the terrain's substance and the residual pockets of space above and below its imposed surfaces (Figure 4.6). "Woven Terrain" offered the students an opportunity to initiate a design project with an architectural construct as a primary guide to inform the disposition of territorial boundaries among a situational environment. While

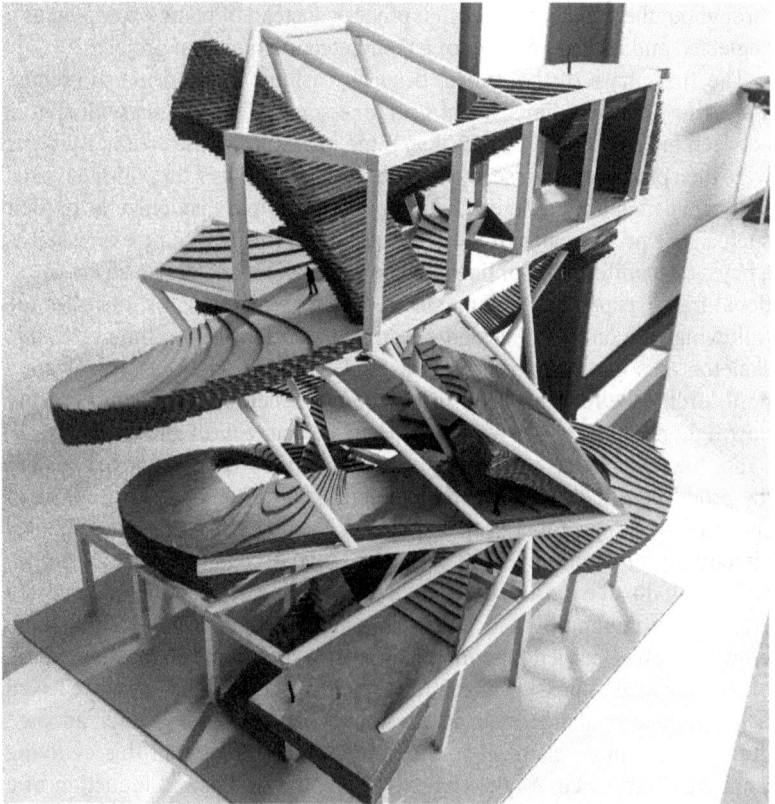

Figure 4.6 "Woven Terrain" final physical model by student Seong Joon Park

this project incited students to reconsider architecture among, within, and/ or beyond the earth by activating topography as the authoritative element to direct spatial flows, the students often struggled to maintain a descriptive design language for their final proposal when uniting the accompanied topographical substances with their tectonic framework assemblies.

Concluding remarks

Designing a memorable experience involves developing a working conversation between site and architecture by recognising and appreciating potential cooperative interactions among all built and natural entities, as opposed to placing emphasis on the static characteristics of autonomous elements that reside over a given field. Each project described earlier requested the students to reconsider how they might announce, engage, and involve the ground as an essential and active participant throughout the architectural design process. Students were persuaded to imagine, manipulate, and reconfigure a designed site in various manners to harmoniously collaborate with an interceding tectonic framework of an architectural establishment. Collectively, the projects encouraged students to reevaluate the territorial bounds between the built and natural settings of a situational environment by interpreting, and representing, the earth as a negotiable plane and/or malleable substance through distinct methodological procedures. Ultimately, the students were invited to consider architecture as a mediatory agent of design, instead of as a foreign object preoccupied with capturing the atmospheric conditions of the sky, and equally acknowledge the site as an accommodating and fluid body to better guide their design decisions.

The four variations of the project presented alternatives to activate the site as a plastic environment, dynamic in its ability to respond and inform operational manoeuvers to announce architecture incessantly throughout the design process. Independently, these design exercises encouraged students to conceptualise and represent the earth's mass through a variety of materials and procedures, including the aggregation of components, as a homogenous body, the assembly of additive contours, and as a responsive body to an established architectural act. Through an examination of students' work for successive design exercises (Figure 4.7), it was observed that the lessons provided by these introductory exercises encouraged students to consider architecture as a volumetric organisation of spatial configurations collaboratively engaged with its environment throughout the design process, within, along, and beyond the earth's atmospheric conditions.

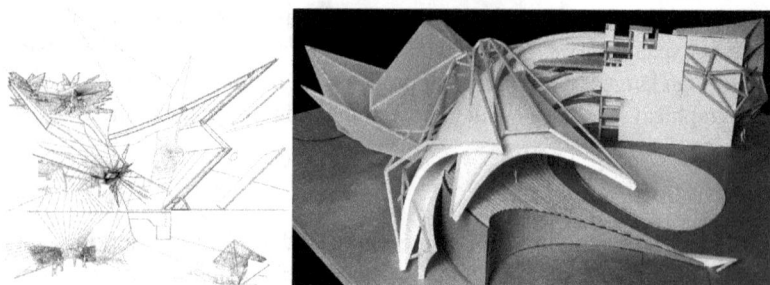

Figure 4.7 Examples of subsequent design projects by second-year students Casey
Stamm (left) and Camden Hochgesang (right)

Notes

1 Gyorgy Kepes, *The New Landscape of Art and Science* (Chicago: Paul Theobald
  and Company, 1963), 204.
2 Ibid.
3 Ibid., 205.
4 Tim Ingold, *Lines: A Brief History* (New York: Routledge, 2007), 39–71.
5 Tim Ingold, *The Life of Lines* (New York: Routledge, 2015), 15–26.
6 Gevork Hartoonian, *Architecture and Spectacle: A Critique* (Farnham Surrey,
  England: Ashgate Publishing, 2012), 5.
7 David Leatherbarrow, "Building In and Out of Place," *Architectural Design,
  Special Issue: Constructions: An Experimental Approach to Intensely Local
  Architectures* 85, no. 2 (March/April 2015): 24–9.
8 Lars Spuybroek, "Experience, Tectonics and Continuity," in *The Architecture of
  Continuity: Essays and Conversations*, ed. Lars Spuybroek (The Netherlands:
  NAI010 Publishers Publishing, 2011), 12–31.
9 Ibid.
10 Ibid.
11 Bernard Cache, *Earth Moves: The Furnishing of Territories* (Cambridge: MIT
   Press, 1995), 10–11.
12 David Leatherbarrow, "Topographical Premises," *Journal of Architectural Education* 57, no. 3 (February 2004): 70–3.
13 Ibid.
14 Ibid.
15 Ilka Ruby and Andreas Ruby, *Groundscapes: The Rediscovery of the Ground in
   Contemporary Architecture* (Barcelona: Gustavo Gili, 2006), 9–30.
16 Vittorio Gregotti, "Address to the New York Architectural League, October
   1982," *Section A* 1, no. 1 (February/March 1983), 8.
17 Kenneth Frampton and John Cava, *Studies in Tectonic Culture: The Poetics of
   Construction in Nineteenth and Twentieth Century Architecture* (Cambridge:
   MIT Press, 1995), 8.
18 Ruby and Ruby, *Groundscapes*, 71.
19 Ibid., 33.

20 David Leatherbarrow, *Uncommon Ground: Architecture, Technology, and Topography* (Cambridge: MIT Press, 2000), 25–70.
21 Leatherbarrow, "Topographical Premises," 70–3.
22 Ibid.
23 Leatherbarrow, *Uncommon Ground*, 25–70.
24 Tomà Berlanda, *Architectural Topographies* (New York: Routledge, 2014), 4.
25 Stanford Anderson, "Modern Architecture and Industry: Peter Behrens, The AEG and Industrial Design," *Oppositions* 21, Summer (1980), 83.
26 Gottfried Semper, *Style in the Technical and Tectonic Arts; or Practical Aesthetics* (Los Angeles: Getty Research Institute, 2004), 109.
27 Ibid., 725.
28 Frampton and Cava, *Studies in Tectonic*, 16.
29 Gevork Hartoonian, *Ontology of Construction: On Nihilism of Technology in Theories of Modern Architecture* (New York: Cambridge University Press, 1997), 40.
30 Robin Evans, *The Projective Cast: Architecture and its Three Geometries* (Cambridge, MA: MIT Press, 1995), 179.
31 Francesco Cacciatore, *The Wall as Living Place: Hollow Structural Forms in Louis Kahn's Work* (Siracusa, Italy: Lettera Ventidue, 2016), 19.
32 Juan González, José Castellón and Pierluigi D'Acunto, "Stereotomic Models in Architecture" (paper presented at the annual meeting for CAADence, Budapest, 2016), 177–84.
33 Lars Spuybroek, *The Sympathy of Things: Ruskin and the Ecology of Design* (The Netherlands: V2_NAI Publishing, 2009), 7–10.

Bibliography

Aldallal, Enis, Husam AlWaer, and Soumyen Bandyopadhyay. *Site and Composition: Design Strategies in Architecture and Urbanism*. New York: Routledge, 2016.

Anderson, Paul, and David Salomon. *The Architecture of Patterns*. New York: W. W. Norton and Company Inc., 2010.

Anderson, Stanford. "Modern Architecture and Industry: Peter Behrens, The AEG and Industrial Design." *Oppositions* 21 (Summer, 1980): 83.

Baudoin, Genevieve. *Interpreting Site: Studies in Perception, Representation, and Design*. New York: Routledge, 2015.

Benjamin, Andrew. *Architectural Projections*. Australia: RMIT University Press, 2012.

Berlanda, Tomà. *Architectural Topographies*. New York: Routledge, 2014.

Cacciatore, Francesco. *The Wall as Living Place: Hollow Structural Forms in Louis Kahn's Work*. Siracusa, Italy: Lettera Ventidue, 2016.

Cache, Bernard. *Earth Moves: The Furnishing of Territories*. Cambridge, MA: The MIT Press, 1995.

Clark, Andrew H. *Diderot's Part: Aesthetics and Physiology*. London, UK: Routledge Publishers, 2018.

Di Mari, Anthony. *Conditional Design: An Introduction to Elemental Architecture*. The Netherlands: BIS Publishers, 2014.

Di Mari, Anthony, and Nora Yoo. *Operative Design: A Catalogue of Spatial Verbs*. The Netherlands: BIS Publishers, 2012.

Evans, Robin. *The Projective Cast: Architecture and Its Three Geometries*. Cambridge, MA: The MIT Press, 1995.

Foged, Isak W., and Marie Frier Hvejsel, eds. *Reader: Tectonics in Architecture*. Aalborg, Denmark: Aalborg University Press, 2018.

Frampton, Kenneth, and John Cava. *Studies in Tectonic Culture: The Poetics of Construction in Nineteenth and Twentieth Century Architecture*. Cambridge, MA: The MIT Press, 1995.

González, Juan, José Castellón, and Pierluigi D'Acunto. "Stereotomic Models in Architecture." Paper presented at the *Annual Meeting for CAADence*, Budapest, 2016.

Gregotti, Vittorio. "The Exercise of Detailing." *Casabella*, June, 1983.

Hartoonian, Gevork. *Architecture and Spectacle: A Critique*. Farnham Surrey, England: Ashgate Publishing, 2012.

Hartoonian, Gevork. *Crisis of the Object: The Architecture of Theatricality*. New York: Routledge, 2006.

Hartoonian, Gevork. *Modernity and Its Other: A Post-Script to Contemporary Architecture*. College Station, Texas: Texas A&M University Press, 1998.

Hartoonian, Gevork. *Ontology of Construction: On Nihilism of Technology in Theories of Modern Architecture*. New York: Cambridge University Press, 1997.

Hornstein, Shelley. *Losing Site: Architecture, Memory, and Place*. New York: Routledge, 2011.

Ingold, Tim. *The Life of Lines*. New York: Routledge, 2015.

Ingold, Tim. *Lines: A Brief History*. New York: Routledge, 2007.

Kanekar, Aarati. *Architecture's Pretexts: Spaces of Translation*. New York: Routledge, 2015.

Kepes, Gyorgy. *Module, Proportion, Symmetry, Rhythm*. Chicago: George Braziller, 1966.

Kepes, Gyorgy. *The New Landscape in Art and Science*. Chicago: Paul Theobald and Company, 1963.

Leatherbarrow, David. "Building in and Out of Place." *Architectural Design, Special Issue: Constructions: An Experimental Approach to Intensely Local Architectures* 85, no. 2, edited by Michael Hensel and Christian Hermansen Cordua (March/April, 2015): 24–9.

Leatherbarrow, David. "Topographical Premises." *Journal of Architectural Education* 57, no. 3 (February, 2004): 70–3.

Leatherbarrow, David. *Uncommon Ground: Architecture, Technology, and Topography*. Cambridge, MA: The MIT Press, 2000.

Mateo, Josep Lluís, and Florian Sauter, eds. *The Four Elements and Architecture: Earth, Water, Air, Fire*. New York: Actar Publishers, 2014.

McCreight, Tim. *The Syntax of Objects*. Brunswick, Maine: Brynmorgen Press, 2009.

Nesbitt, Kate, ed. *Theorizing a New Agenda for Architecture: An Anthology of Architectural Theory 1965–1995*. New York: Princeton Architecture, 1996.

Ruby, Ilka, and Andreas Ruby. *Groundscapes: The Rediscovery of the Ground in Contemporary Architecture*. Barcelona: Gustavo Gili, 2006.

Semper, Gottfried. *Style in the Technical and Tectonic Arts or Practical Aesthetics*. Los Angeles: Getty Research Institute, 2004.

Spuybroek, Lars, ed. *The Architecture of Continuity: Essays and Conversations*. The Netherlands: NAI010 Publishers Publishing, 2011.

Spuybroek, Lars. *Research and Design: The Architecture of Variation*. London: Thames and Hudson, 2009.

Spuybroek, Lars. *The Sympathy of Things: Ruskin and the Ecology of Design*. The Netherlands: V2_NAI Publishers, 2009.

Spuybroek, Lars. *Textile Tectonics: Research and Design*. The Netherlands: NAI Publishing, 2011.

Toadvine, Ted, and Lester Embree. *Merleau-Ponty's Reading of Husserl*. New York: Springer Publishing, 2002.

Warren, Samuel. *Stereotomy: Problems in Stone Cutting in Four Classes*. Cambridge: John Wiley and Son, 1875.

Wilson, Peter. *Themes V: Informing the Object*. London: Architectural Association Publishing, 1986.

5 Strategies for nurturing evaluative judgement in design students

Charlie Smith

Introduction

Evaluative judgement has been defined as the capability to make decisions about the quality of one's own work and that of others.[1] Design students need to develop evaluative judgement so they can progress through their work constructively during self-directed study time, critically discuss work with their peers and become increasingly independent learners – active agents in determining quality in their work, as opposed to being reliant on assessment by others.[2] It is an equally important skill for students to develop in the context of design practice, where creative initiative and autonomy are valuable attributes. Graduates need to be able to self-monitor the quality of their work, identify their ongoing learning needs,[3] and understand what constitutes standards of performance in their field,[4] not least for when they are required to appraise and comment on the work of others.[5] For example, in a study of graduates employed in the computer graphics industry, the definition of "professionalism" used by Paquette et al. was that graduates must be able "to evaluate their own work and behaviour in the context of a workplace environment and the demands of the industry."[6] Robinson describes creativity as involving two interweaving process of being generative and evaluative, and he argues that helping people to understand and manage how they leaven generating ideas with making judgements about them is a pivotal aspect of creative development.[7]

However, as Sadler highlights, qualitative judgement cannot be reduced to the application of a set of measures or formal procedures; it needs to be learnt through experience.[8] Elwood and Klenowski stress the fundamental importance of the development of communities of shared understanding in relation to assessment and propose that students need access to the wide range of assessment activities employed by tutors and to the shared understandings of how tutors make their judgements.[9] It is common practice in contemporary higher education for students' work to be graded against explicit standards but, as Orr and Shreeve highlight, in order to construct and agree on such standards students and tutors must actively engage with them through dialogue within communities of practice. Furthermore, they maintain that engaging students in the creative assessment conversation contributes to the overarching learning goal of helping each student "develop their own evaluative gaze."[10]

This chapter presents two strategies for nourishing evaluative judgement: student peer review and the use of exemplars to generate discussion around standards and dimensions of quality. Both have been trialed in an architecture programme at a post ninety-two UK university but are pertinent to other design-orientated programmes. With many curricula already densely populated, it was considered important to identify methods that relate the development of learners' judgements to established features of the curriculum and not add new ones.[11]

Theoretical frame for nurturing evaluative judgement

Learning in design disciplines occurs primarily through studio tutorials (also known as desk crits) and usually take place as one-to-one conversations or small-group discussions. They are interspaced periodically with design reviews (also known as crits and juries) which are formative or summative appraisals in which students present their design work to a panel of reviewers. These panels usually include other tutors in the programme and guest critics from practice outside the university. The student's peers will also observe the session during which feedback is received in the form of verbal commentary. This approach of dialogic tutorials interspaced with design reviews frequently constitutes the signature pedagogy of the disciplines.[12] Learning centres around conversations amongst tutors, students and their peers within the same and different cohorts, through which participants are enculturated into studio practices.[13] As such, it strongly aligns design pedagogy with a socio-constructivist approach in which student and tutor are involved in a social process of collaborative interaction through loops of dialogue.[14] In socio-constructivist pedagogy, Palincsar describes discourse as the primary means of cognitive development, expertise as facility with such discourse, and learning occurring through interaction, negotiation and collaboration.[15]

With learning already occurring in a context characterised by conversations amongst tutors, students and their peers, it follows that the processes of nurturing evaluative judgement should similarly align with a socio-constructivist approach: a model in which participants actively engage in co-construction and meaning making through dialogue.[16] It is an approach that also depends upon students' sense of agency within their learning.[17]

This chapter considers two methods through which design students can develop the ability to make evaluative judgements by actively engaging within the learning environment in processes that are centred around discourse amongst participants. Central to fostering students' evaluative expertise is the construction of a dialogic process that takes place in a generative learning environment where feedback is repositioned as a feature of interactive, collectivist student engagement,[18] and opportunities are provided to observe and discuss how self-generated judgements of work compare to those of others.[19] One way to facilitate this is for students to collaboratively review the work of their peers.

Developing evaluative judgement through peer review

It has been argued that peer evaluation is a cornerstone of professionalism and that the process can facilitate subsequent employee evaluation skills, such as where recent graduates are required to appraise the work of others.[20] Several attributes of peer review nurture evaluative judgement, including the development of critical thinking and clarity around what constitutes quality,[21] enhancing meta-cognitive skills in differentiating and justifying,[22] formative application of assessment criteria to project work,[23] and encouraging a more self-critical view of students' own work.[24] However, this approach is not without potential obstacles. For example, student motivation may be reduced where peer reviews have only a formative dimension.[25] Additionally, students can find it difficult to be critical of their peers, especially where social relationships have been constructed.[26] This could create challenging circumstances in a studio environment, where students often form strong social bonds.

Students in the third and final year of their undergraduate architecture degree at a post ninety-two UK university were invited to participate in peer reviews where they would take the place of tutors as the critics in design reviews.[27] From the overall cohort of seventy-one students, eight volunteered to participate in the reviews and are the 'participants' referred to in this study.

The reviews were held in the design studio, where the participants were working on their final comprehensive design project (a twenty-week module). In keeping with the established format of design reviews in the programme, each participant exhibited their current formative drawings and models and stood in front of their work to present it to the reviewers, who were sitting in a loose semicircle in front of them. The panel in traditional reviews typically comprises only two or three critics, but in these peer sessions the seven other participants were the panel. Holding the peer sessions in a familiar format was deliberate. Sadler proposes that students need to be involved in appraisal judgements that are as similar to those of their tutors as feasible.[28] This arrangement also aligned with optimal models for peer review proposed by both Nicol and van den Berg et al.[29] Each student described their project to the peer reviewers, who then asked questions and gave verbal feedback to the presenting student. The tutor sat at the back as a facilitator, intervening only to draw each review to a close and move the group on to the next. Two peer review sessions were held. The first took place halfway through the module with a second session two weeks later, giving the participants the opportunity to reflect on the feedback they had received from their peers and incorporate it into their work.

The peer reviews were evaluated via a short answer questionnaire that was emailed to participants following the second session. It consisted of eleven open questions exploring aspects such as the following: how did the reviews contribute to the participants' learning, whether they found it difficult to be critical of their colleagues' work and whether they had learnt anything not directly related to their project. All participants completed the questionnaire. Their responses were studied anonymously through relational content analysis to identify key concepts in the data and the responses associated with each.[30]

The analysis revealed that the experience of the peer reviews had facilitated the participants' creative thinking and developed their confidence in making critical judgements about their peers' work – a key facet of evaluative judgement – as these responses demonstrate:

> During the reviews a lot of the students were bouncing ideas off each other at quite a fast rate. I feel that by doing this it encouraged us to use our creative thinking at a quicker rate.
>
> > Participant One

> I was confident that I had gained enough understanding . . . that I felt capable of offering constructive critical comment.
>
> > Participant Six

> Yes, [I learnt] the ability to give constructive criticism in a way that is applicable to the fellow person is valuable.
>
> > Participant Four

Nicol highlights that group peer review engages students in evaluating a range of work of differing quality produced to the same brief and that they thereby make comparative judgements across these projects.[31] This process nurtures students' understanding of standards of quality. Research also suggests that peer review engages students in multiple acts of evaluation and critical judgement about both the other students' work and, in different ways, about their own.[32] Zhu and Carless propose that a key feature of this research is that composing commentary for peers may strengthen students' own inner feedback processes, enhancing their ability to calibrate inner and external feedback – a process that thereby refines their judgement capabilities.[33] Three-quarters of participants in this study describe applying the critique process to their own design work as a result of the peer review sessions. Having to analyse other students' projects in order to provide them with developmental feedback facilitated greater evaluation of the participants' own work, with an identifiable increase in their self-critical analysis, as the following responses illustrate:

> I did find that after critiquing someone else's work, I asked myself if the points made were pertinent to my own project.
>
> Participant Six

> I feel it has helped in that its [sic] allowed me to become more self-critical of my own work . . . I learned a better understanding of how to critique work, which is likely to help in future design projects.
>
> Participant One

> After the peer reviews when working on my design I thought about each aspect of the design with a critical mind asking 'do I need this here?' and 'what does this contribute to my project, is it positive or negative?'
>
> Participant Seven

Indeed, it has been argued that when reviewing the work of others, students invariably make comparative evaluations with their own and consider ways of improving it.[34] In developing their ability to make evaluative judgements, students need to be able to discern quality (what is good and what is not) and to identify it in the work they produce themselves – a process evidenced in Participant Seven's response (earlier) which indicates the student making self-critical reflections in the context of quality.[35] Nicol contends that evaluative judgement is the cornerstone of critical thinking,[36] and these responses evidence its emergence as a result of the peer design reviews. Increased levels of self-critique are an integral part of developing autonomy and creative initiative – skills that are increasingly important in an uncertain and more rapidly evolving employment landscape.

Although the participants were briefed on the nature of feedback to be provided in these reviews – critically constructive and developmental – the module's assessment criteria were not deployed to structure their evaluations of their peers' work. Tai et al. suggest that students comparing work to criteria and standards leads to a better understanding of quality and that with a more explicit focus on evaluative judgements, students can glean what constitutes quality in other's work and transfer it to their own – as illustrated in the responses given earlier.[37] However, others question whether the process of developing students' own conceptions of quality is enhanced when they are not given preformulated criteria, but where instead criteria emerge through the appraisals.[38] Furthermore, Sadler cautions that focusing on criteria encourages students to think about qualities, or particularities, within the work as opposed to overall quality.[39]

One aspect of nurturing evaluative judgement that is particularly relevant for design disciplines is the understanding that quality can be perceived in different ways and manifest in different forms. Involvement in the peer review process deepened the participants' appreciation of different opinions and perspectives around their own work and that of their peers, as the following responses illustrate:

> In a traditional review there is normally around [two] or at the most, [three] people there. In the peer reviews we had a small group which resulted in a range of different opinions which we don't necessarily get in a traditional review.
>
> Participant Eight

> When you review other people's work you seem to be able to pick up on . . . different ways that they can tackle their work.
>
> Participant Five

> The peer reviews offered a different viewpoint on my design project which highlighted some issues which otherwise I don't think I would have seen.
>
> Participant Seven

Austerlitz and Aravot propose that students' emotional responses to discussions around their work are some of the most important processes through which they evaluate their studio encounters and interpret meaning from dialogue and therefore exert significant influence on their learning.[40] Steen-Utheim and Wittek further identify the significance of emotional and relational support to students' dialogic feedback recipience and emphasise that uptake of feedback is likely to be enhanced where participants are within a supportive environment.[41] An important facet of a cooperative learning context is, therefore, trust amongst all participants.[42] This was present during the peer reviews, as the following participants confirm:

> I felt we had a positive rapport amongst the group which allowed each member to not take any critical comments personally and understand that we were all in the position of wanting to help the fellow students.
>
> Participant Four

> Initially I didn't know what to expect, I thought the peer reviews would be more formal than they actually were. When realising how informal the situation was it made us more relaxed and we were encouraged to speak up and voice our opinions.
>
> Participant One

> The fact that you know the person allowed me personally to give some stronger worded feedback than if it was a stranger.
>
> Participant Seven

Peer review can be conducted anonymously with the reviewers' feedback delivered to the reviewee via the virtual learning environment (VLE) or an online platform, and some research suggests that students consider anonymity in the process to be important.[43] In contrast, the peer reviews in this study replicated the arrangement of traditional reviews, with students delivering verbal feedback directly through face-to-face discussion in the design studio. Delivering feedback in this way has potential to create tension amongst peers. Indeed, while two participants described initially feeling cautious about giving critical feedback, they said this diminished as the first session progressed. The remaining participants did not find making critical comments on their peers' work awkward. The positive rapport within the peer review process identified by Participant Four (given earlier) is particularly noteworthy. This is significant because Winstone and Carless identify an important aspect of the peer feedback process being verbal dialogue amongst the participants; this is because it gives the receiver the opportunity to explain the intentions underpinning their work, to clarify or negotiate meaning with their peers, or to ask those providing the feedback to elaborate or justify their comments.[44] Crucially, they suggest that negotiating feedback messages in this way can enable students to think more deeply about the nature of quality. A study of peer feedback with both written commentary and verbal dialogue found that students consider the verbal dialogue to be an important part of the feedback process as it enhances evaluative skills.[45] As such, the dialogic forum of the peer reviews would appear to contribute positively to developing the ability to make decisions about the quality of others' work and therefore in nurturing the evaluative judgement of all involved.

Using exemplars to nurture evaluative judgement

Sadler observes that tutors' evaluative judgements and concepts of quality are honed by their repeated exposure to myriad submissions of work.[46] Similarly, therefore, he argues that students themselves should be involved in appraising multiple examples.[47] Design students often ask to see examples of coursework, not least so that they can improve their understanding of the work they are being asked to produce. Winstone and Carless suggest that sharing and analysing exemplars of work can be a useful way to support students in developing an understanding of what quality work looks like as well as clarifying assessment rubrics. It offers students concrete embodiments of work of different levels of performance and leads to students appreciating both how quality can be achieved and how it can take on different forms.[48] The latter point is particularly pertinent to design programmes which are characterised by a divergent process of learning and development in project work.

Exemplars can include samples of previous coursework submissions or analogous work such as precedents. Their use is particularly suited to creative programmes in other ways. For example, in-class discussion around images and models can be facilitated within the session itself whereas an essay would need to be read in advance. However, there are potential challenges with using exemplars including the depth of engagement achieved and the influence of student–tutor power dynamics on the development of evaluative judgement capabilities.[49]

In recent years, the module leader in the second year of the same undergraduate architecture programme from which the peer review study's participants were drawn provided students with examples of previous submissions for their first-semester design project. They were uploaded onto the VLE at the start of term and, although their presence was highlighted to students, there was no further discussion of them. It soon became evident that students were not engaging effectively with this valuable resource. Therefore, in the 2018–19 academic year the decision was taken to use teaching sessions with the cohort to discuss the exemplars at length, including numerous examples for each submission component. These in-class discussions, a combination of lectures and studio workshops which occurred approximately halfway through the coursework, included a synopsis of the ideas underlying each submission and debate around quality in terms of strengths, weaknesses and key features in each. The discussion was loosely structured around the module's assessment criteria,[50] introducing the students to standards and dimensions of quality associated with each example of the coursework – a key aspect of developing evaluative judgement.[51]

The module surveys at this institution ask students to evaluate their course using similar, but fewer, questions than the National Student Survey (NSS) – an independent evaluation that all final-year undergraduate students in UK universities are asked to complete. Both surveys evaluate overall satisfaction, how well staff explain things, whether the module or course is intellectually stimulating, whether the criteria used for marking have been made clear in advance, and the adequacy of academic support provided. The NSS consistently shows that students across all disciplines are least satisfied with the issue of assessment; furthermore, satisfaction is lower than average in architecture.[52]

Significantly, after discussions around exemplars were introduced to the second-year cohort, satisfaction around assessment increased considerably; it scored joint top in the module survey alongside the question that asked how good staff were at explaining things, with both achieving eighty-seven percent 'agree' or 'strongly agree.' The margin of lead over the score for the next highest response was considerable – ten percent 'agree' or 'strongly agree.' In sharp contrast, the third-year cohort (that had not discussed exemplars in this manner) scored the question in the NSS relating to marking criteria at sixty-three percent. Although no direct correlation can be proven, this increase in the second-year cohort's awareness and understanding of the criteria used to assess their work implies a corresponding increase in their cognisance of the processes through which their tutors undertake evaluative judgement of their work. In pedagogic studies, there are a number of interacting variables that influence research outcomes, such as natural variations between successive cohorts, making conclusions difficult to draw.[53] However, although again no conclusive correlation can be drawn, it was disappointing to discover that the mean module component marks for the cohort in which exemplars were extensively discussed showed no increase in student attainment over those of the previous year.

The following academic year, the module leader extended the in-class dialogue to include more detailed discussion around how the module's assessment criteria could be applied to the exemplars. A study by Bell, Mladenovic and Price found that exemplars can play a role in supporting students to make sense of assessment criteria, and they advocate formal activities such as small-group open-forum class discussion around such resources.[54] The in-class dialogue with the second-year cohort was framed as a series of questions that tutors might ask themselves when assessing the work. For example, for the first assessment criterion, "Design development – record of design development process," the following questions were put to the students:

Where have the ideas underpinning the scheme come from?
What is the quality and originality of the design concept for the project?
How creatively has that concept been explored?
What is the quality and scope of developmental work (design journals, plus bound sheets)?

For the second assessment criterion, "Design resolution," the following questions were posed:

How creatively and thoughtfully has the concept been translated into the proposed scheme, through a coherent thought process?
What is the depth and thoroughness with which ideas have been translated into a credible and creative proposal?
What is the level of ambition and complexity evident within the project?
How comprehensively have the functions of the project been considered and then worked out?

The students were shown a series of projects produced for that module component by students from previous years. The exemplars were discussed in the context of these questions, providing a frame of reference for their analysis. The objective was not only to make characteristics of quality visible to the students but also to illuminate tutors' tacit ways of interpreting and applying assessment criteria when making evaluative judgement over that quality, without which – Handley and Williams suggest – students are limited in their ability to learn from exemplars and improve their own work.[55] In contrast to students passively looking at exemplars on the VLE in their own time, this active dialogue between students and design tutors about the exemplars and assessment criteria embeds analysis of them within the socio-constructivist interpretive pedagogy of the discipline. It creates a learning space in which exemplars become the means to interpret, agree and contest understandings of quality, how it manifests in these artefacts, and the dimensions against which quality is evaluated, to arrive at shared meanings within a community of practice.[56]

Curiously, while the module evaluation score for how well staff explained things remained consistent following the introduction of additional discussion around how assessment criteria might be applied to the exemplars (increasing by one percent 'agree' or 'strongly agree'), the score for whether the marking criteria had been made clear actually fell by almost ten percent to seventy-nine percent 'agree' or 'strongly agree.' Furthermore, there was a small decrease in the mean module component marks for the cohort. Possible reasons for this are discussed later.

When selecting exemplars, a choice must be made – whether to present a range of submissions that demonstrate a spectrum of standards or to use only stronger ones. In this study, the examples of previous work were all graded sixty-five percent or above. Carless and Chan used high standard exemplars on the basis that students might learn more from work of excellent quality.[57] However, Joughin et al. propose that strong exemplars could act as anchors, biasing students' toward making more favourable evaluative judgements when they compare their own work to them; interestingly, they also suggest that having students evaluate the work of their peers before their own may mitigate the impact of these anchoring heuristics.[58]

Some propose using a range of exemplars in order to demonstrate different standards of quality.[59] Henderson et al. argue it would be more beneficial to choose exemplars that stimulate conversations around issues of quality, as opposed to stand-alone examples of differing quality, and that multiple exemplars may be more useful in demonstrating the variety of possible responses and the contingent nature of evaluative judgement.[60] This is particularly pertinent in subjective disciplines such as creative programmes. Similarly, it has been argued that to achieve the greatest benefit, exemplars should be chosen that represent features of quality more broadly applicable to the discipline and not just for a given task.[61] Sadler proposes that the minimum number of exemplars required relates to the number of criteria used, as this influences the different ways in which quality can be constructed, but in any event more than one is required to appreciate that quality can be realised in alternative ways.[62]

Another consideration is when to introduce exemplars to the students. Carless et al. reverse the dominant trend in exemplars literature by suggesting that students commence their own work before analysing that of others, their rationale being that students may be more cognitively engaged and ready to develop evaluative judgement skills through being able to compare their own evolving work with the exemplars.[63] Tutors may also have concerns that showing examples of previous work or precedent projects will inhibit students' own creative exploration.[64] Introducing exemplars after students have started their task may reduce the tendency for them to adopt surface-level imitation of the exemplars. In this study the exemplars were uploaded to the VLE at the start of the module but were only discussed with the students around the midway point.

Tai et al. caution that exemplars require some commentary for students to use them to full advantage in developing their evaluative judgement but, to benefit the most, there needs to be a careful balance between students' active participation in identifying quality in samples of work and the descriptions of quality and articulation of judgements made by the tutor.[65] This has implications for the way tutors structure in-class discussions around exemplars.

Where exemplars are drawn from coursework by previous cohorts there is an opportunity to enhance class discussion by involving the students who produced the work in the session. Arnold and Headley term this approach "bringing in the author" and describe how it facilitates discussion on the developmental processes underpinning the work – not just the finished product – and allows students to understand how the author felt throughout the project.[66] Given the emphasis placed on process as well as resolution in design subjects, this approach aligns strongly with learning objectives.

Discussion

On the basis that social learning is an important way of developing and clarifying thinking, Winstone and Carless propose that peer dialogue – such as that which occurs during peer review – is consistent with the principles of socio-constructivist learning.[67] This, as was argued earlier, should be central the processes of nurturing evaluative judgement given that the signature pedagogy of the discipline is already characterised by conversation and dialogue to facilitate meaning making. The environment created for the peer reviews in this study had a supportive quality, which enabled students to feel confident in making critical judgements of each other's work.

Crucially, in the context of nurturing evaluative judgement, the process of reviewing their peers' work helped the students develop deeper self-evaluation of their own. Furthermore, the process enhanced their appreciation that quality can manifest through different approaches – a key dimension of evaluative judgement in subjective and divergent fields such as design. The overarching objective of both methods studied in this chapter – student peer review and discussion around exemplars – is to foster an environment in which students' self-evaluation becomes a mode of learning. Orr and Shreeve propose that greater emphasis be placed on peer review in the evaluative judgement of art and design projects, reasoning that it can be a useful way to bring students into the community of practice around assessment and encourage them to think like a practitioner.[68]

Winstone and Carless suggest that tutor feedback often does not connect with students due to lack of understanding over assessment criteria or standards; they argue that positioning students as peer reviewers places them in a role that prompts them to engage with the assessment criteria and helps them to perceive the qualities exhibited in coursework.[69] As such, not only does the process facilitate students' development of evaluative judgement, it also facilitates their interpretation of both module assessment criteria and of tutor's feedback on summative assessment of their own work, which will be of wider benefit to them in subsequent modules. It is a multidimensional enhancement of their assessment literacy.

In the study described in this chapter, the discussions with students over exemplars of previous submissions relevant to their ongoing coursework appeared to have significantly increased their understanding of the modules' assessment criteria, as demonstrated by the increase in module evaluation scores. It could reasonably be inferred that there was a corresponding increase in students' understanding of the processes of evaluative judgement that tutors undertake when assessing such coursework, as this formed a key element of the in-class discussions. In a study where exemplars were made available to students on the VLE but not discussed in class, Handley and Williams found that students' difficulty in understanding assessment criteria limited their ability to learn from the examples. They suggest that the main benefits of learning through exemplars accrue through in-class dialogue.[70] Indeed, Carless and Chan propose that class dialogue is probably the most important element in using exemplars to support students in the development of an appreciation of the nature of quality. They state that discussion should be focused on eliciting students' views and that they should be given time and space to identify and refine their evaluative judgements before the imposition of the tutor's view.[71] The process of developing capability in evaluative judgement therefore demands a shift in the power dynamic, moving away from judgements made by tutors toward a much overlooked aspect of the learning process – self-critique and analysis by students themselves. Students need participative experience in making judgements, interrogating and discussing them,[72] which is why simply showing exemplars or making them available on a VLE is not enough.

The fluctuation in module evaluation scores on the question of clarity of marking criteria and the small decrease in the mean module component marks are worthy of further comment. Although the module evaluation score actually decreased by nine percent following the introduction of additional discussion around how the module's assessment criteria might be applied to exemplars, this is unlikely to be the only causal factor in the outcome of the module surveys. In fact, the second-year cohort where the exemplars were discussed scored higher than the third-year cohort where they had not. Also, this was not a longitudinal study (where the same cohort of students is observed as they move through the different levels of the programme) and therefore, as noted earlier, factors such as natural variations between successive cohorts can influence research outcomes and make overarching conclusions difficult to draw. As such, these fluctuations in the module evaluation scores must be treated with a degree of caution.

Significantly, this was the first time the students had encountered in-depth discussions around exemplar work and the framing of that discussion around the application of the module's assessment criteria in evaluating different aspects and manifestations of quality in that work. As with the introduction of any new concept or approach to learning, students need both time and opportunity to absorb and develop their understanding of it. Tai et al. conceptualise building evaluative judgement as an iterative cycle, not unlike the design process itself, in which making comparisons with the work of others deepens understanding of quality, which in turn enhances making subsequent comparisons.[73] It has therefore been argued that students should have repeated opportunities to be active participants in the formulation of critical judgements.[74] For this reason, it is important that events like peer review and discussion around exemplars should not be undertaken in isolation. A more robust approach would be to chart the module evaluation scores relating to clarity of assessment criteria through successive modules, and indeed successive cohorts, in which exemplars are repeatedly deployed to discuss dimensions of quality and the evaluative judgement of that quality with students. This would be a valuable avenue for further research. Orr and Shreeve argue that it is crucial that students graduate knowing how to evaluate their work and that the more they are given the space and time to develop their own evaluative judgement skills, the better equipped they are to thrive after graduation.[75]

Whilst this chapter has discussed ways to nurture evaluative judgement as two independent strategies, these approaches can be combined. For example, Elwood and Klenowski describe a study in which exemplars were evaluated by students as a preparation exercise for peer reviews; the purpose of this exercise was to facilitate understanding of assessment criteria, provide insight into their interpretation, and address potential dissonance between students' and tutors' perceptions of assessment by building common understandings through negotiation.[76]

Design disciplines are inherently divergent in their nature; once given a project brief, students move along their own unique trajectories to create their artefacts. As such, students must embrace uncertainty and ambiguity in their learning, where the resolution of any project is unknown at the outset.[77] An important benefit of the use of exemplars, therefore, is to demonstrate to students the range of responses they might work toward, thereby alleviating some of the anxiety that characterises the start of a new project.[78]

Appraising students' evaluative judgement

It has been argued that educators should be concerned with determining the quality of students' evaluative judgement, which could be achieved through reflecting on the qualities of judgements made and the thought processes and justifications used.[79] This would have the effect of turning a tacit aspect of the hidden curriculum into an explicit one: one that is evaluated itself, if not assessed. However, evaluating this process could prove challenging. Dawson suggests that articulating the ways in which evaluative judgements are made by experts may be very difficult,[80] a view illustrated by the adage no doubt familiar to many design academics: "I cannot really describe what quality is, but I know it when I see it."[81] But this does not mean that it should not be attempted. Lodge et al. argue that illusions of competence over the ability to conduct evaluative judgements may mean that the students most in need of rectifying misalignment between evaluative judgements of their work and its actual quality are those least likely to recognise it.[82]

Whilst recognising that there is a fine line between worthwhile formative evaluation and rewarding students through marks, Winstone and Carless propose that awarding a percentage of an overall grade for participation in peer review would be a pragmatic option, due to the fact that student engagement in a task is often facilitated through there being some summative assessment weighting attached to it.[83]

One approach in peer design reviews would be for the tutor facilitating the session to appraise each students' contributions to the process;[84] this can be captured on a rubric, with the tutor providing feedback to each student on the quality of their evaluative judgements of their peers. Another approach would be for the student being reviewed to appraise the feedback from their peers. Arguably, however, it would be challenging for students to meaningfully appraise the verbal commentary they are receiving in the forum of the open discussion typical of design reviews. In fact, the verbal delivery in peer design reviews is likely to be significant in nurturing evaluative judgement; van den Berg et al. found that oral as opposed to written feedback facilitated peers' explanations of their judgements, and students' interactions more often assumed an evaluative mode.[85] Furthermore, students may not be able to appraise the quality of evaluative judgement as effectively as a tutor.

Students could be asked to submit their own evaluations in class with the exemplars exhibited in a studio session or lecture. Alternatively, exemplars could be presented on the VLE and then evaluated by the students during self-directed study. The tutor can then assess the scope and quality of students' evaluative critique, such as the extent to which they demonstrate the ability to articulate and defend their judgements. A significant advantage of this approach is that in mirroring the assessment method followed by tutors, students gain a greater understanding of what they often perceive as an opaque and ambiguous process, especially if they are tasked with evaluating exemplars using the criteria that they will be assessed against.[86] This would, however, place additional demands on tutors' time and workload, against which any perceived advantages would need to be weighed. An alternative approach would be for students to peer-assess or self-assess their evaluations of exemplars; this would have the advantage of continuing the process of developing their ability to make decisions about the quality of one's own work or that of others – the very definition of evaluative judgement.[87]

Conclusions

It has been argued that learners must be equipped not just for what they need to be able to do in their course, but for the multiplicity of challenges they will face after graduation,[88] and that nurturing evaluative judgement should be an explicit learning objective in higher education.[89] Orr and Shreeve argue that through discursive assessment practices students rehearse the way that designers and artists think, through which a shared social meaning can evolve and their evaluative judgement in relation to creative work can develop. They also assert that working with explicit modes of visual and verbal communication facilitates access to shared understandings of standards and expectations within a community of practice.[90]

There are advantages and disadvantages, as well as similarities and differences, to both methods discussed in this chapter. As Carless et al. highlight, in both peer review and appraising exemplars of previous submissions, students are evaluating the work of someone else, as well as comparing that performance with their own.[91] However, exemplars have usually been produced by someone outside the immediate learning context, and the process therefore lacks the benefit of its creator receiving feedback, as occurs during peer review. In peer review, however, standards of quality in the work being discussed cannot be controlled or benchmarked in the way they can with exemplars chosen by tutors. However, exposing students to a range of quality can benefit their understanding of quality and standards. Whereas exemplars need careful consideration of the student–tutor power dynamic when discussing quality, peer review fundamentally overturns the power relation.[92] By immersing students in the process of formulating feedback, peer review engages them in critical judgements about the work of others; they experience the process for themselves, as opposed to it being imposed on them. This has implications for how exemplars are used; it must be a participatory experience and not one in which the tutor identifies what is good and bad.

Tai et al. propose that curricula may better induct learners into a discipline by providing them with opportunities to participate in the processes of making judgements and discussing standards and criteria.[93] Liu and Carless argue that students should analyse illustrative exemplars to clarify such notions of quality, which themselves can include the work of their peers.[94] So, although this chapter discusses two different means of nurturing evaluative judgement in design students, they should not be considered in isolation as peer review is just one form of exemplar work that can facilitate this. As Sadler contends, "Exemplars convey messages that nothing else can."[95]

Notes

1 Rola Ajjawi, Joanna Tai, Phillip Dawson and David Boud, "Conceptualising Evaluative Judgement for Sustainable Assessment in Higher Education," in *Developing Evaluative Judgement in Higher Education*, ed. David Boud et al. (Abingdon: Routledge, 2018), 7.

2 Joanna Tai, Rola Ajjawi, David Boud, Philip Dawson and Ernesto Pandero, "Developing Evaluative Judgement: Enabling Students to Make Decisions about the Quality of Work," *Higher Education* 76 (2018): 478, accessed January 16, 2019, doi:10.1007/s10734-017-0220-3; Naomi E. Winstone, Robert A. Nash, Michael Parker and James Rowntree, "Supporting Learners' Agentic Engagement with Feedback: A Systematic Review and a Taxonomy of Recipience Processes," *Educational Psychologist* 52, no. 1 (2017): 18, accessed September 5, 2018, doi:10.1080/00461520.2016.1207538.

3 Gordon Joughin, David Boud and Phillip Dawson, "Threats to Student Evaluative Judgement and Their Management," *Higher Education Research and Development* 38, no. 2 (2019). 537, accessed November 21, 2018, doi 10.1080/07294360.2018.1536967.

4 Tai et al., "Developing Evaluative Judgement," 468.

5 David Nicol, Avril Thomson and Caroline Breslin, "Rethinking Feedback Practices in Higher Education: A Peer Review Perspective," *Assessment and Evaluation in Higher Education* 39, no. 1 (2014): 119, accessed January 17, 2019, doi: 10.1080/02602938.2013.795518; Keith Topping, "Peer Assessment Between Students in Colleges and Universities," *Review of Educational Research* 68, no. 3 (1998): 256, accessed January 30, 2019, doi:10.3102/00346543068003249.

6 Andrew Paquette, Gabriel Reedy and Stylianos Hatzipanagos, "Race Cars and the Hellbox: Understanding the Development of Proficiency Among Digital Art Students," *Art, Design and Communication in Higher Education* 15, no. 1 (2016): 25, cited in Susan Orr and Alison Shreeve, *Art and Design Pedagogy in Higher Education: Knowledge, Values and Ambiguity in the Creative Curriculum* (Abingdon: Routledge, 2018), 103.

7 Ken Robinson, *Out of Our Minds: The Power of Being Creative*, Third Edition (Chichester, UK: Wiley, 2017), 130–1.

8 D. Royce Sadler, "Formative Assessment and the Design of Instructional Systems," *Instructional Science* 18 (1989): 139, accessed September 13, 2018, doi:10.1007/BF00117714.

9 Jannette Elwood and Val Klenowski, "Creating Communities of Shared Practice: The Challenges of Assessment Use in Learning and Teaching," *Assessment and Evaluation in Higher Education* 27, no. 3 (2002): 254 and 246, accessed January 17, 2020, doi:10.1080/02602930220138606.

10 Susan Orr and Alison Shreeve, *Art and Design Pedagogy in Higher Education: Knowledge, Values and Ambiguity in the Creative Curriculum* (Abingdon: Routledge, 2018), 138.

11 Tai et al., "Developing Evaluative Judgement," 478.

12 Susan Orr, Mantz Yorke and Bernadette Blair, "'The Answer Is Brought about from within You': A Student-Centred Perspective on Pedagogy in Art and Design," *International Journal of Art and Design Education* 33, no. 1 (2014): 38, accessed October 1, 2019, doi:10.1111/j.1476-8070.2014.12008.x; Ashraf M. Salama, *Spatial Design Education: New Directions for Pedagogy in Architecture and Beyond* (Farnham, Surry: Ashgate, 2015), 77–9; Bernadette Blair,

"Does the Studio Crit Still Have a Role to Play in 21st-Century Design Education and Student Learning?," in *Enhancing Curricula: Contributing to the Future, Meeting the Challenges of the 21st Century in the Disciplines of Art, Design and Communication*, ed. Allan Davies (London: Centre for Learning and Teaching in Art and Design, 2006), 107.

13 Inger Mewburn, "Lost in Translation: Reconsidering Reflective Practice and Design Studio Pedagogy," *Arts and Humanities in Higher Education* 11, no. 4 (2012), accessed January 9, 2020, doi:10.1177/1474022210393912.

14 Susan Askew and Caroline Lodge, "Gifts, Ping-Pong and Loops: Linking Feedback and Learning," in *Feedback for Learning*, ed. Susan Askew (Abingdon: Routledge, 2000), 11–13.

15 A. Sullivan Palincsar, "Social Constructivist Perspectives on Teaching and Learning," *Annual Review of Psychology* 49, no. 1 (1998): 361 and 365, accessed January 7, 2020, doi:10.1146/annurev.psych.49.1.345.

16 Naomi Winstone and David Carless, *Designing Effective Feedback Processes in Higher Education: A Learning-Focused Approach* (Abingdon: Routledge, 2020), 12.

17 Berry O'Donovan, Chris Rust and Margaret Price, "A Scholarly Approach to Solving the Feedback Dilemma in Practice," *Assessment and Evaluation in Higher Education* 41, no. 6 (2016): 939, accessed June 28, 2019, doi:10.1080/0 2602938.2015.1052774.

18 David Carless, "Sustainable Feedback and the Development of Student Self-Evaluative Capacities," in *Reconceptualising Feedback in Higher Education: Developing Dialogue with Students*, ed. by Stephen Merry et al. (Abingdon: Routledge, 2013), 113; David Boud and Elizabeth Molloy, "Rethinking Models of Feedback for Learning: The Challenge of Design," *Assessment and Evaluation in Higher Education* 38, no. 6 (2013): 706, accessed January 23, 2018, doi: 10.1080/02602938.2012.691462.

19 Christina Johnson and Elizabeth Molloy, "Building Evaluative Judgement Through the Process of Feedback," in *Developing Evaluative Judgement in Higher Education*, ed. David Boud et al. (Abingdon: Routledge, 2018), 167.

20 Nicol et al., "Rethinking Feedback Practices," 119; George A. Marcoulides and Mark G. Simkin, "Evaluating Student Papers: The Case for Peer Review," *Journal of Education for Business* 67, no. 2 (1991): 82–3, accessed February 4, 2019, doi:10.1080/08832323.1991.10117521.

21 Topping, "Peer Assessment Between," 255 and 259.

22 Keith J. Topping, "The Effectiveness of Peer Tutoring in Further and Higher Education: A Typology and Review of the Literature," *Higher Education* 32 (1996): 324, accessed January 17, 2019, doi:10.1007/BF00138870.

23 Winstone and Carless, *Designing Effective Feedback*, 121.

24 David Nicol, "Guiding Principles for Peer Review: Unlocking Learners' Evaluative Skills," in *Advances and Innovations in University Assessment and Feedback*, ed. Carolin Kreber et al. (Edinburgh: Edinburgh University Press, 2014), 204.

25 Keith Pond, Rehan Ul-Haq and Winnie Wade, "Peer Review: A Precursor to Peer Assessment," *Innovations in Education and Training International* 32, no. 4 (1995): 322, accessed February 12, 2019, doi:10.1080/1355800950320403.

26 Nancy Falchikov, "Peer Feedback Marking: Developing Peer Assessment," *Innovations in Education and Training International* 32, no. 2 (1995): 184, accessed September 7, 2012, doi:10.1080/1355800950320212.

118   *Charlie Smith*

27 Charlie Smith, "When Students Become Critics: Reviewing Peer Reviews in Theory and Practice," *Charrette* 6, no. 1 (2020): 71–92, accessed May 13, 2020, www.ingentaconnect.com/content/arched/char; Charlie Smith, "Evaluating Architecture Students' Perspective of Learning in Peer Reviews" (paper presented at DRS // CUMULUS 2nd International Conference for Design Education Researchers, Oslo, May 14–17, 2013), vol. 1: 343–55. The papers provide a full description of the peer review study. This chapter focuses in depth on the role of peer review in developing critical analysis and evaluative judgement skills. It incorporates unpublished data and new analysis from the study which relate specifically to these aspects of the peer reviews.

28 D. Royce Sadler, "Beyond Feedback: Developing Student Capability in Complex Appraisal," *Assessment and Evaluation in Higher Education* 35, no. 5 (2010): 541, accessed July 18, 2011, doi:10.1080/02602930903541015.

29 Nicol, "Guiding Principles," 209; Ineke van den Berg, Wilfried Admiraal and Albert Pilot, "Peer Assessment in University Teaching: Evaluating Seven Course Designs," *Assessment and Evaluation in Higher Education* 31, no. 1 (2006): 34, accessed July 18, 2011, doi:10.1080/02602930500262346.

30 Catherine Marshall and Gretchen B. Rossman, *Designing Qualitative Research* (London: SAGE Publications, 2011), 161.

31 Nicol, "Guiding Principles," 204–5.

32 Nicol et al., "Rethinking Feedback Practices," 116.

33 Qiyun Zhu and David Carless, "Dialogue Within Peer Feedback Processes: Clarification and Negotiation of Meaning," *Higher Education Research and Development* 37, no. 4 (2018): 895, accessed October 15, 2019, doi:10.1080/07294360.2018.1446417.

34 Nicol, "Guiding Principles," 204; D. Royce Sadler, "Indeterminacy in the Use of Preset Criteria for Assessment and Grading," *Assessment and Evaluation in Higher Education* 34, no. 2 (2009): 177, accessed September 11, 2018, doi:10.1080/02602930801956059.

35 Joughin et al., "Threats to Student," 538.

36 Nicol, "Guiding Principles," 201.

37 Tai et al., "Developing Evaluative Judgement," 475.

38 Nicol, "Guiding Principles," 208; Sadler, "Indeterminacy in the Use," 176.

39 D. Royce Sadler, "Ah! . . . So That's 'Quality'," in *Assessment: Case Studies, Experience and Practice from Higher Education*, ed. Peter Schwartz and Graham Webb (London: Kogan Page, 2002), 135.

40 Noam Austerlitz and Iris Aravot, "The Emotional Structure of the Student-Tutor Relationship in the Design Studio," in *Enhancing Curricula: Contributing to the Future, Meeting the Challenges of the 21st Century in the Disciplines of Art, Design and Communication*, ed. Allan Davies (London: Centre for Learning and Teaching in Art and Design, 2006), 94–5.

41 Anna Steen-Utheim and Anne Line Wittek, "Dialogic Feedback and Potentialities for Student Learning," *Learning, Culture and Social Interaction* 15 (2017): 28, October 18, 2019, doi:10.1016/j.lcsi.2017.06.002.

42 Boud and Molloy, "Rethinking Models of Feedback," 709.

43 Nicol et al., "Rethinking Feedback Practices," 109.

44 Winstone and Carless, *Designing Effective Feedback*, 140.

45 Zhu and Carless, "Dialogue Within Peer," 890–1.

46 Sadler, "Beyond Feedback," 540.

47 Sadler, "Indeterminacy in the Use," 177.

48 Winstone and Carless, *Designing Effective Feedback*, 81.
49 David Carless, Kennedy Kam Ho, Jessica To, Margaret Lo and Elizabeth Barrett, "Developing Students' Capacities for Evaluative Judgement Through Analysing Exemplars," in *Developing Evaluative Judgement in Higher Education*, ed. David Boud et al. (Abingdon: Routledge, 2018), 114.
50 D. Royce Sadler, "Assuring Academic Achievement Standards: From Moderation to Calibration," *Assessment in Education: Principles, Policy and Practice* 20, no. 1 (2013): 10–1, accessed January 23, 2019, doi:10.1080/0969594X.2012.714742.
51 Tai et al., "Developing Evaluative Judgement," 471.
52 David Vaughan and Mantz York, "'I Can't Believe it's Not Better': The Paradox of NSS Scores for Art and Design," *Higher Education Academy* (2009): 8, accessed January 23, 2019, www.heacademy.ac.uk/system/files/nss-arts-design.pdf. Note: Analysis of 2017 NSS data by the author showed that whilst the mean satisfaction score for Assessment and Feedback has increased in Architecture programmes, it is still below the national mean for all subjects.
53 Karen Handley and Lindsay Williams, "From Copying to Learning: Using Exemplars to Engage Students with Assessment Criteria and Feedback," *Assessment and Evaluation in Higher Education* 36, no. 1 (2011): 102, accessed January 27, 2020, doi:10.1080/02602930903201669.
54 Amani Bell, Rosina Mladenovic and Margaret Price, "Students' Perceptions of the Usefulness of Marking Guides, Grade Descriptors and Annotated Exemplars," *Assessment and Evaluation in Higher Education* 38, no. 7 (2013): 776 and 780, accessed January 30, 2020, doi:10.1080/02602938.2012.714738.
55 Handley and Williams, "From Copying to Learning," 104.
56 Orr and Shreeve, *Art and Design Pedagogy*, 129–30.
57 David Carless and Kennedy Kam Ho Chan, "Managing Dialogic Use of Exemplars," *Assessment and Evaluation in Higher Education* 42, no. 6 (2017): 932–3, accessed January 27, 2020, doi:10.1080/02602938.2016.1211246.
58 Joughin et al., "Threats to Student," 545.
59 Such as: Nicol, "Guiding Principles," 213; and Sadler, "Beyond Feedback," 544, for example.
60 Michael Henderson, Michael Phillips and Tracii Ryan, "Designing for Technology-Enabled Feedback," in *Developing Evaluative Judgement in Higher Education*, ed. David Boud et al. (Abingdon: Routledge, 2018), 120.
61 Tai et al., "Developing Evaluative Judgement," 476.
62 Sadler, "Formative Assessment," 128.
63 Carless et al., "Developing Students' Capacities," 109.
64 Sadler, "Formative Assessment," 128; Handley and Williams, "From Copying to Learning," 98.
65 Tai et al., "Developing Evaluative Judgement," 476–7.
66 Lydia Arnold and Jane Headley, "How Can We Work With Exemplars? Collated Ideas from an Institutional Community of Practice," *SEDA Educational Developments* 20, no. 3 (2019): 25.
67 Winstone and Carless, *Designing Effective Feedback*, 103.
68 Orr and Shreeve, *Art and Design Pedagogy*, 137.
69 Winstone and Carless, *Designing Effective Feedback*, 122.
70 Handley and Williams, "From Copying to Learning," 104.
71 Carless and Chan, "Managing Dialogic Use," 935–9.
72 Sadler, "Beyond Feedback," 244.

73 Joanna Hong-Meng Tai, Benedict J. Canny, Terry P. Haines and Elizabeth K. Molloy, "The Role of Peer-Assisted Learning in Building Evaluative Judgement: Opportunities in Clinical Medical Education," *Advances in Health Sciences Education* 21 (2016): 671, accessed January 22, 2019, doi:10.1007/s10459-015-9659-0.
74 Tai et al., "Developing Evaluative Judgement," 472.
75 Orr and Shreeve, *Art and Design Pedagogy*, 137.
76 Elwood and Klenowski, "Creating Communities," 249.
77 Orr and Shreeve, *Art and Design Pedagogy*, 63.
78 Arnold and Headley, "How Can We Work," 24.
79 Tai et al., "Developing Evaluative Judgement," 478.
80 Phillip Dawson, "Exemplars, Feedback and Bias: How Do Computers Make Evaluative Judgements?" in *Developing Evaluative Judgement in Higher Education*, ed. David Boud et al. (Abingdon: Routledge, 2018), 100.
81 Sadler, "Ah! . . . So That's 'Quality'," 135.
82 Jason M. Lodge, Gregor Kennedy and John Hattie, "Understanding, Assessing and Enhancing Student Evaluative Judgement in Digital Environments," in *Developing Evaluative Judgement in Higher Education*, ed. David Boud et al. (Abingdon: Routledge, 2018), 73.
83 Winstone and Carless, *Designing Effective Feedback*, 121–2.
84 Nicol, "Guiding Principles," 203; Nicol et al., "Rethinking Feedback Practices," 109; David Boud, Ruth Cohen and Jane Sampson, "Peer Learning and Assessment," in *Peer Learning in Higher Education*, ed. David Boud et al. (London: Kogan Page, 2001), 76.
85 van den Berg et al., "Peer Assessment," 34.
86 Tai et al., "The Role of," 668. Topping, "Peer Assessment," 256; Sadler, "Formative Assessment," 135.
87 Ajjawi, Tai, Dawson and Boud, "Conceptualising Evaluative Judgement," 7.
88 David Boud and Rebeca Soler, "Sustainable Assessment Revisited," *Assessment and Evaluation in Higher Education* 41, no. 3 (2016): 401, accessed January 23, 2019, doi:10.1080/02602938.2015.1018133.
89 Joughin et al., "Threats to Student," 539.
90 Orr and Shreeve, *Art and Design Pedagogy*, 158.
91 Carless et al., "Developing Students' Capacities," 114.
92 Nicol, "Guiding Principles," 210.
93 Tai et al., "Developing Evaluative Judgement," 473.
94 Ngar-Fun Liu and David Carless, "Peer Feedback: The Learning Element of Peer Assessment," *Teaching in Higher Education* 11, no. 3 (2006): 281, accessed February 15, 2011, doi:10.1080/13562510600680582.
95 Sadler, "Ah! . . . So That's 'Quality'," 136.

Bibliography

Ajjawi, Rola, Joanna Tai, Phillip Dawson, and David Boud. "Conceptualising Evaluative Judgement for Sustainable Assessment in Higher Education." In *Developing Evaluative Judgement in Higher Education*, edited by David Boud, Rola Ajjawi, Phillip Dawson, and Joanna Tai, 7–17. Abingdon: Routledge, 2018.

Arnold, Lydia, and Jane Headley. "How Can We Work with Exemplars? Collated Ideas from an Institutional Community of Practice." *SEDA Educational Developments* 20, no. 3 (2019): 24–7.

Askew, Susan, and Caroline Lodge. "Gifts, Ping-Pong and Loops: Linking Feedback and Learning." In *Feedback for Learning*, edited by Susan Askew, 1–17. Abingdon: Routledge, 2000.

Austerlitz, Noam, and Iris Aravot. "The Emotional Structure of the Student-Tutor Relationship in the Design Studio." In *Enhancing Curricula: Contributing to the Future, Meeting the Challenges of the 21st Century in the Disciplines of Art, Design and Communication*, edited by Allan Davies, 91–106. London: Centre for Learning and Teaching in Art and Design, 2006.

Bell, Amani, Rosina Mladenovic, and Margaret Price. "Students' Perceptions of the Usefulness of Marking Guides, Grade Descriptors and Annotated Exemplars." *Assessment and Evaluation in Higher Education* 38, no. 7 (2013): 769–88. Accessed January 30, 2020. doi:10.1080/02602938.2012.714738.

Blair, Bernadette. "Does the Studio Crit still Have a Role to Play in 21st-Century Design Education and Student Learning?" In *Enhancing Curricula: Contributing to the Future, Meeting the Challenges of the 21st Century in the Disciplines of Art, Design and Communication*, edited by Allan Davies, 107–20. London: Centre for Learning and Teaching in Art and Design, 2006.

Boud, David, Ruth Cohen, and Jane Sampson. "Peer Learning and Assessment." In *Peer Learning in Higher Education*, edited by David Boud, Ruth Cohen, and Jane Sampson, 67–81. London: Kogan Page, 2001.

Boud, David, and Elizabeth Molloy. "Rethinking Models of Feedback for Learning: The Challenge of Design." *Assessment and Evaluation in Higher Education* 38, no. 6 (2013): 698–712. Accessed January 23, 2018. doi:10.1080/02602938.2012.691462.

Boud, David, and Rebeca Soler. "Sustainable Assessment Revisited." *Assessment and Evaluation in Higher Education* 41, no. 3 (2016): 400–13. Accessed January 23, 2019. doi:10.1080/02602938.2015.1018133.

Carless, David. "Sustainable Feedback and the Development of Student Self-Evaluative Capacities." In *Reconceptualising Feedback in Higher Education: Developing Dialogue with Students*, edited by Stephen Merry, Margaret Price, David Carless, and Maddalena Taras, 113–22. Abingdon: Routledge, 2013.

Carless, David, and Kennedy Kam Ho Chan. "Managing Dialogic Use of Exemplars." *Assessment and Evaluation in Higher Education* 42, no. 6 (2017): 930–41. Accessed January 27, 2020. doi:10.1080/02602938.2016.1211246.

Carless, David, Kennedy Kam Ho Chan, Jessica To, Margaret Lo, and Elizabeth Barrett. "Developing Students' Capacities for Evaluative Judgement Through Analysing Exemplars." In *Developing Evaluative Judgement in Higher Education*, edited by David Boud, Rola Ajjawi, Phillip Dawson, and Joanna Tai, 108–16. Abingdon: Routledge, 2018.

Dawson, Phillip. "Exemplars, Feedback and Bias: How do Computers Make Evaluative Judgements?" In *Developing Evaluative Judgement in Higher Education*, edited by David Boud, Rola Ajjawi, Phillip Dawson, and Joanna Tai, 99–107. Abingdon: Routledge, 2018.

Elwood, Jannette, and Val Klenowski. "Creating Communities of Shared Practice: The Challenges of Assessment Use in Learning and Teaching." *Assessment and Evaluation in Higher Education* 27, no. 3 (2002): 243–56. Accessed January 17, 2020. doi:10.1080/02602930220138606.

Falchikov, Nancy. "Peer Feedback Marking: Developing Peer Assessment." *Innovations in Education and Training International* 32, no. 2 (1995): 175–87. Accessed September 7, 2012. doi:10.1080/1355800950320212.

Handley, Karen, and Lindsay Williams. "From Copying to Learning: Using Exemplars to Engage Students with Assessment Criteria and Feedback." *Assessment and Evaluation in Higher Education* 36, no. 1 (2011): 95–108. Accessed January 27, 2020. doi:10.1080/02602930903201669.

Henderson, Michael, Michael Phillips, and Tracii Ryan. "Designing for Technology-Enabled Feedback." In *Developing Evaluative Judgement in Higher Education*, edited by David Boud, Rola Ajjawi, Phillip Dawson, and Joanna Tai, 117–26. Abingdon: Routledge, 2018.

Johnson, Christina, and Elizabeth Molloy. "Building Evaluative Judgement through the Process of Feedback." In *Developing Evaluative Judgement in Higher Education*, edited by David Boud, Rola Ajjawi, Phillip Dawson, and Joanna Tai, 166–75. Abingdon: Routledge, 2018.

Joughin, Gordon, David Boud, and Phillip Dawson. "Threats to Student Evaluative Judgement and Their Management." *Higher Education Research and Development* 38, no. 3 (2019): 537–49. Accessed November 21, 2018. doi:10.1080/0729 4360.2018.1544227.

Liu, Ngar-Fun, and David Carless. "Peer Feedback: The Learning Element of Peer Assessment." *Teaching in Higher Education* 11, no. 3 (2006): 279–90. Accessed February 15, 2011. doi:10.1080/13562510600680582.

Lodge, Jason M., Gregor Kennedy, and John Hattie. "Understanding, Assessing and Enhancing Student Evaluative Judgement in Digital Environments." In *Developing Evaluative Judgement in Higher Education*, edited by David Boud, Rola Ajjawi, Phillip Dawson, and Joanna Tai, 70–8. Abingdon: Routledge, 2018.

Marcoulides, George A., and Mark G. Simkin. "Evaluating Student Papers: The Case for Peer Review." *Journal of Education for Business* 67, no. 2 (1991): 80–3. Accessed February 4, 2019. doi:10.1080/08832323.1991.10117521.

Marshall, Catherine, and Gretchen B. Rossman. *Designing Qualitative Research*. London: SAGE Publications, 2011.

Mewburn, Inger. "Lost in Translation: Reconsidering Reflective Practice and Design Studio Pedagogy." *Arts and Humanities in Higher Education* 11, no. 4 (2012): 363–79. Accessed January 9, 2020. doi:10.1177/1474022210393912.

Nicol, David. "Guiding Principles for Peer Review: Unlocking Learners' Evaluative Skills." In *Advances and Innovations in University Assessment and Feedback*, edited by Carolin Kreber, Charles Anderson, Noel Entwistle, and Jan McArthur, 197–224. Edinburgh: Edinburgh University Press, 2014.

Nicol, David, Avril Thomson, and Caroline Breslin. "Rethinking Feedback Practices in Higher Education: A Peer Review Perspective." *Assessment and Evaluation in Higher Education* 39, no. 1 (2014): 102–22. Accessed January 17, 2019. doi:10. 1080/02602938.2013.795518.

O'Donovan, Berry, Chris Rust, and Margaret Price. "A Scholarly Approach to Solving the Feedback Dilemma in Practice." *Assessment and Evaluation in Higher Education* 41, no. 6 (2016): 938–49. Accessed June 28, 2019. doi:10.1080/0260 2938.2015.1052774.

Orr, Susan, and Alison Shreeve. *Art and Design Pedagogy in Higher Education: Knowledge, Values and Ambiguity in the Creative Curriculum.* Abingdon: Routledge, 2018.

Orr, Susan, Mantz Yorke, and Bernadette Blair. "'The Answer Is Brought about from within You': A Student-Centred Perspective on Pedagogy in Art and Design." *International Journal of Art and Design Education* 33, no. 1 (2014): 32–45. Accessed October 1, 2019. doi:10.1111/j.1476-8070.2014.12008.x.

Palincsar, A. Sullivan. "Social Constructivist Perspectives on Teaching and Learning." *Annual Review of Psychology* 49, no. 1 (1998): 345–75. Accessed January 7, 2020. doi:10.1146/annurev.psych.49.1.345.

Paquette, Andrew, Gabriel Reedy, and Stylianos Hatzipanagos. "Race Cars and the Hellbox: Understanding the Development of Proficiency Among Digital Art Students." *Art, Design and Communication in Higher Education* 15, no. 1 (2016): 7–34. Cited in Orr, Susan, and Alison Shreeve. *Art and Design Pedagogy in Higher Education: Knowledge, Values and Ambiguity in the Creative Curriculum.* Abingdon: Routledge, 2018.

Pond, Keith, Rehan Ul-Haq, and Winnie Wade. "Peer Review: A Precursor to Peer Assessment." *Innovations in Education and Training International* 32, no. 4 (1995): 314–23. Accessed February 12, 2019. doi:10.1080/1355800950320403.

Robinson, Ken. *Out of Our Minds: The Power of Being Creative.* Third Edition. Chichester, UK: Wiley, 2017.

Sadler, D. Royce. "Ah! . . . So That's 'Quality'." In *Assessment: Case Studies, Experience and Practice from Higher Education,* edited by Peter Schwartz and Graham Webb, 130–6. London: Kogan Page, 2002.

Sadler, D. Royce. "Assuring Academic Achievement Standards: From Moderation to Calibration." *Assessment in Education: Principles, Policy and Practice* 20, no. 1 (2013): 5–19. Accessed January 23, 2019. doi:10.1080/0969594X.2012.714742.

Sadler, D. Royce. "Beyond Feedback: Developing Student Capability in Complex Appraisal." *Assessment and Evaluation in Higher Education* 35, no. 5 (2010): 535–50. Accessed July 18, 2011. doi:10.1080/02602930903541015.

Sadler, D. Royce. "Formative Assessment and the Design of Instructional Systems." *Instructional Science* 18 (1989): 119–44. Accessed September 13, 2018. doi:10.1007/BF00117714.

Sadler, D. Royce. "Indeterminacy in the Use of Preset Criteria for Assessment and Grading." *Assessment and Evaluation in Higher Education* 34, no. 2 (2009): 159–79. Accessed September 11, 2018. doi:10.1080/02602930801956059.

Salama, Ashraf M. *Spatial Design Education: New Directions for Pedagogy in Architecture and Beyond.* Farnham, Surry: Ashgate, 2015.

Smith, Charlie. "Evaluating Architecture Students' Perspective of Learning in Peer Reviews." Paper presented at *DRS//CUMULUS 2nd International Conference for Design Education Researchers,* Oslo, May 14–17, 2013, Vol. 1, 343–55.

Smith, Charlie. "When Students Become Critics: Reviewing Peer Reviews in Theory and Practice." *Charrette* 6, no. 1 (2020): 71–92. Accessed May 13, 2020. www.ingentaconnect.com/content/arched/char.

Steen-Utheim, Anna, and Anne Line Wittek. "Dialogic Feedback and Potentialities for Student Learning." *Learning, Culture and Social Interaction* 15 (2017): 18–30. Accessed October 18, 2019. doi:10.1016/j.lcsi.2017.06.002.

Tai, Joanna Hong-Meng, Rola Ajjawi, David Boud, Philip Dawson, and Ernesto Pandero. "Developing Evaluative Judgement: Enabling Students to Make Decisions about the Quality of Work." *Higher Education* 76 (2018): 467–81. Accessed January 16, 2019. doi:10.1007/s10734-017-0220-3.

Tai, Joanna Hong-Meng, Benedict J. Canny, Terry P. Haines, and Elizabeth K. Molloy. "The Role of Peer-Assisted Learning in Building Evaluative Judgement: Opportunities in Clinical Medical Education." *Advances in Health Sciences Education* 21 (2016): 659–76. Accessed January 22, 2019. doi:10.1007/s10459-015-9659-0.

Topping, Keith J. "The Effectiveness of Peer Tutoring in Further and Higher Education: A Typology and Review of the Literature." *Higher Education* 32 (1996): 321–45. Accessed January 17, 2019. doi:10.1007/BF00138870.

Topping, Keith J. "Peer Assessment Between Students in Colleges and Universities." *Review of Educational Research* 68, no. 3 (1998): 249–76. Accessed January 30, 2019. doi:10.3102/00346543068003249.

van den Berg, Ineke, Wilfried Admiraal, and Albert Pilot. "Peer Assessment in University Teaching: Evaluating Seven Course Designs." *Assessment and Evaluation in Higher Education* 31, no. 1 (2006): 19–36. Accessed July 18, 2011. doi:10.1080/02602930500262346.

Vaughan, David, and Mantz York. "'I Can't Believe It's Not Better': The Paradox of NSS Scores for Art and Design." *Higher Education Academy*, 2009. Accessed January 23, 2019. www.heacademy.ac.uk/system/files/nss-arts-design.pdf.

Winstone, Naomi E., and David Carless. *Designing Effective Feedback Processes in Higher Education: A Learning-Focused Approach.* Abingdon: Routledge, 2020.

Winstone, Naomi E., Robert A. Nash, Michael Parker, and James Rowntree. "Supporting Learners' Agentic Engagement with Feedback: A Systematic Review and a Taxonomy of Recipience Processes." *Educational Psychologist* 52, no. 1 (2017): 17–37. Accessed September 5, 2018. doi:10.1080/00461520.2016.1207538.

Zhu, Qiyun and David Carless. "Dialogue within Peer Feedback Processes: Clarification and Negotiation of Meaning." *Higher Education Research and Development* 37, no. 4 (2018): 883–97. Accessed October 15, 2019. doi:10.1080/07294360.2018.1446417.

Conclusions

Charlie Smith

This book is premised on the concept that challenging orthodoxy should be an intrinsic dimension of creative pedagogy and that teaching in design disciplines should itself be characterised by original and imaginative methods that break new ground, underpinned by critical thinking. Teaching creativity places an onus on teaching creatively. To paraphrase Robinson and Aroncia, properly conceived teaching itself is a form of art.[1] In presenting innovative practices, implemented and reflected upon by each chapter's authors, this book aims to inspire readers to adapt them into their own teaching or to adopt similarly progressive methods. The teaching and learning strategies described in the case studies are applicable across different spatial design disciplines and are all transferable. The approaches described in the context of an architecture programme, for example, can be applied to students' creative explorations in landscape architecture, interior architecture and urban design, amongst others.

Teaching and learning strategies must proactively embrace the increasing diversity of students arriving into higher education, including but not limited to their gender, race, ethnicity, ability, beliefs, interests and age. Chapters 1 and 2 both recognise this diversity and discuss different approaches to facilitating students' transition into university and supporting their learning at the outset of their programme. Griesel and Fourie-Malherbe posit that design education can fail to recognise and take sufficient account of the wide range of students' preparedness for design education. In response, they propose a framework for enhancing skill sets to assist students cope more effectively with moving from school to higher education by developing their design skills in progressive ways. They highlight the importance of skill sets that are critical in dealing with real-world situations, such as such as problem-solving, interpersonal and linguistic skills, and of authentic contextual, collaborative and creative teaching and learning environments, including outside of the studio. Reflecting on students' experiences of a learning context in which the framework was implemented, they conclude that the modal agency meaning-making process within the framework facilitated students' skills and knowledge development by linking the understanding of theoretical knowledge concepts and their real-life application.

Griesel and Fourie-Malherbe's chapter addresses a fundamental aspect of design learning – the iterative development of creative thinking and self-efficacy; they propose a step-by-step process to facilitate this, which moves from taking a theoretical concept in design knowledge toward its abstract interpretation as conceptual representation. Significantly, although explored in the context of a landscape architecture programme, the challenge of supporting students from diverse backgrounds, facilitating their transition into higher education learning, and enhancing their design skill sets is common across architecture and allied design fields, and this framework provides a valuable approach through which to do this.

In his chapter on taking writing into the design studio, Tripp acknowledges that his approach might be viewed as controversial, even with hostility, by some. However, one of the central tenets of creative practice is to challenge conventional ways of thinking. Like creative practice, creative teaching and learning can be divergent and split opinion, stimulating debate and critical reflection. Yet nurturing students' abilities to transfer learning between different contexts is a salient issue that faces many design disciplines. Tripp argues that integrating writing into courses that are not traditionally writing-based provides an unconventional approach to abstracting and transferring learning, which develops both writing and critical thinking skills via a mechanism that already exists within students' natural language. To the frustration of their tutors, students often perceive learning within the lecture theatre to be unrelated to their project work in the studio,[2] and this chapter has designed a bridge between these learning environments at the beginning of the course that is both pertinent and applicable to other creative disciples.

Operationalising progressive studio pedagogy requires teachers to be willing to take the initiative and experiment with their learning, teaching and evaluation methods. They then need to reflect on the impact of these innovations, turning the process of critical evaluation to their own teaching strategies to further enhance them. Listening to the student voice can reveal crucial insights in this respect. Chapters 3 and 4 both disrupt strategies of conventional inquiry, confront and unsettle familiar working processes, and provoke alternative methods of creative and critical thinking. In doing so, they formulate a deeper understanding of complex conditions and situations to influence and enrich design approaches in the studio. In this sense, both likewise embody the theme that questioning orthodoxy should be an intrinsic dimension of creative teaching praxis.

Challenging the status quo of design methodology in the studio, van Aswegen introduces a workshop as a disruptive 'plug-in', which explores a human-centred approach by introducing design actions in which students adopt the perspective of the user. She argues that conventional methods can no longer adequately address the complex challenges hidden in design projects and that other ways of immersing students in complex challenges could be instrumental to engaged learning. Students thereby become agents for the fluid and unpredictable scenarios inscribed in those projects. Following the journey of two students through the workshop enables the reading of their individual experiences of the same process; their self-reflection reveals that the different modes of engagement facilitated a deepening of their insights. Whilst unsettling their conventional ways of working, the process enabled unforeseen responses, such as connected design engagement and expressing their experiences in terms of emotional connotations, and emphasises the potential value of a situational human-centred approach. The plug-in workshop as a disruptive agent within a spatial design studio demonstrates one means of introducing alternative forms of inquiry to the design process. Furthermore, although described in the context of interior architecture, van Aswegen's depiction of raising awareness of the contingent and temporal nature of people–environment interaction and people–people relationships, and actively engaging with the dynamic and ephemeral conditions associated with spatial occupation, can equally be applied to architecture, landscape architecture and urban design.

As opposed to the conventional perception of a project's site being a permanent and static condition, Burns envisages it being reinterpreted as an active terrain. Like van Aswegen, he challenges conventional working processes and advocates a departure from prescribed design methodology. Here, though, it is moving away from the traditional sequence of observe, record and respond – and instead investigating opportunities to promote a responsive dialogue between architecture and its environment throughout the design process. Burns has devised a series of projects that act as exercises in stimulating students' reevaluation of boundaries between the built and natural settings of a situational environmental by interpreting and representing the earth as a negotiable plane or malleable substance. The condition of site is common across architecture and allied fields, meaning that his reconsideration of it as a responsive dialogue and facilitator between an intervention and its location is equally salient to landscape architecture and urban design, for example. Burns' objective is to encourage students towards acknowledging site as an accommodating and fluid body, and in doing so he presents a valuable additional dimension to students' repertoire of iterative design processes, one which deepens their creative exploration.

The landscape of graduate employment is changing rapidly and the forms it will take, even within the near future, are uncertain and impossible to foresee. Teaching strategies in all disciplines must prepare their students for graduating into an increasingly unpredictable environment. Design students need to develop evaluative judgement skills during their studies to become independent learners who can think and act with critical judgement. Moreover, it is a crucial skill in design practice where creative initiative, resilience and autonomy are valuable attributes, and graduates need to be capable of self-monitoring quality in their own work and appraising that of others. Chapter 5 argued that developing evaluative judgement should be an explicit learning objective in higher education, not a tacit skill that tutors assume students will develop through osmosis, and that students need repeated opportunities as active agents within the process. The two methods discussed – student peer review and using exemplars to discuss dimensions of quality – facilitate students' creative and critical thinking, increase their understanding of assessment methods, and enhance their appreciation that quality can manifest in different ways. In short, they bring a multitude of values to students' learning within the design studio.

This book exemplifies a variety of ways in which pedagogy in design programmes can adopt innovative and creative methods: ones that support students through their transition into higher education, nurture their creative and critical thinking skills whilst there, and ready them for after they graduate. Crucially, the authors show how these progressive, and in some instances disruptive, learning and teaching methods can be implemented within the framework of existing curricula and studio teaching practices. They can be applied to other creative disciplines, even beyond architecture and allied design fields. Creative teaching, like creative practice, should seek to continually push boundaries. As these chapters demonstrate, this requires teachers to reflect on their practices and strive to develop them with similar imaginative purpose to that they wish to see in their students.

Interest in creative approaches to thinking and learning is extending beyond art and design disciplines. Orr and Shreeve describe how, through its focus on developing students' skills around creativity, resilience and criticality, pedagogy in creative disciplines equips them for twenty-first-century life.[3] Echoing the views of Ken Robinson, described in the Introduction, they propose that creative learning and teaching practices could be usefully transposed into other disciplines – particularly around themes such as student-centred learning, problem-based learning and co-production of knowledge – and they offer models of practice for transdisciplinary contexts.[4] Progressive studio pedagogy has much to offer towards enriching students' learning experiences, both within its allied fields and beyond.

Notes

1 Ken Robinson and Lou Aroncia, *Creative Schools* (London: Penguin Random House, 2016), 100.

2 Barry Maitland and Rob Cowdroy, "Redesigning PBL: Resolving the Integration Problem," in *Problem-Based Learning: Case Studies, Experience and Practice*, ed. Peter Schwartz, Stewart Mennin, and Graham Webb (London: Kogan Page Limited, 2001), 91.
3 Susan Orr and Alison Shreeve, *Art and Design Pedagogy in Higher Education: Knowledge, Values and Ambiguity in the Creative Curriculum* (Abingdon: Routledge, 2018), 157–8.
4 Ibid.

Bibliography

Maitland, Barry, and Rob Cowdroy. "Redesigning PBL: Resolving the Integration Problem." In *Problem-Based Learning: Case Studies, Experience and Practice*, edited by Peter Schwartz, Stewart Mennin, and Graham Webb, 90–7. London: Kogan Page Limited, 2001.

Orr, Susan, and Alison Shreeve. *Art and Design Pedagogy in Higher Education: Knowledge, Values and Ambiguity in the Creative Curriculum*. Abingdon: Routledge, 2018.

Robinson, Ken, and Lou Aroncia. *Creative Schools*. London: Penguin Random House, 2016.

Index

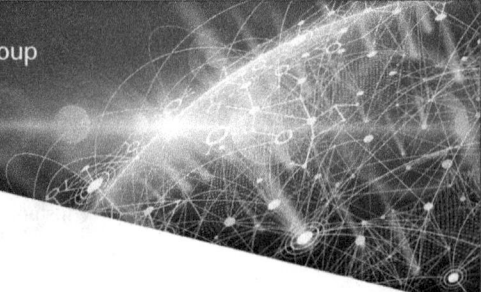

For Product Safety Concerns and Information please contact our EU
representative GPSR@taylorandfrancis.com
Taylor & Francis Verlag GmbH, Kaufingerstraße 24, 80331 München, Germany

www.ingramcontent.com/pod-product-compliance
Lightning Source LLC
Chambersburg PA
CBHW061748270326
41928CB00011B/2417